Caravanning for Beginners

Towing, Buying, Selling & More!

Martin Woodward

Cover photo courtesy of Barefoot Caravans - https://www.go-barefoot.co.uk

1st Edition 2020

ISBN: 978-0-244-55953-3

Enquiries: https://deep-relaxation.co.uk

Contents

Introduction

To begin with, here's a just bit about me.

- I've been driving since 1966

- I passed the IAM in 1971

- I became a driving instructor in 1973. During this period, I attained Grade 6 (top grade) status

- During the following 30 years I built one of the largest and most successful driving schools in South Yorkshire which is still going now (under my name) but with new owners

- In total, during the last 54 years I've driven over 2 million miles across 17 countries

- I've never had a fault accident or insurance claim

- I've never had any points on my licence ever - *and no, they didn't send me a badge or a Unicorn after 50 years!*

- During this time, I've owned numerous caravans and motorhomes and have towed caravans, folding campers and cars on trailers and A-frames literally thousands of miles across Europe

Clever bugger then?

No, not at all, just very careful and very aware of my limitations!

I don't even consider myself to be a super skilful driver like my father was. I'm just boringly careful. But like any human, I make mistakes and would be the first to admit it. There's no such thing as a perfect driver. I guess that I've been pretty lucky to have driven so far without acquiring any penalty points on my licence or to have avoided any insurance claims.

If you haven't already worked it out, I'm also an ancient old git, but one with a lifetime of knowledge and experience to share.

And now I'm going to make a shocking admission - *I don't like towing!* The reasons for this will become apparent as we progress. In fact, I much prefer to drive motorhomes, but they too have many disadvantages so overall, I've concluded that towing a caravan is better for me, and no doubt many others alike.

Why?

Well, size for size there's generally a better level of comfort in a caravan, but most importantly, you will have the car for travelling about in when you reach your destination, and this alone can make a huge difference to your holiday experience.

Why not tow a car?

I've towed cars both on trailers and on A-frames extensively. In the case of the trailers, they need a large area to store them both on sites and at home; plus, there's a load of grief getting the car on and off them - especially in the mud and rain. A-frames are less hassle but are illegal outside of the UK - *the manufacturers will dispute this, and they may well be right but try explaining this to an irate Spanish policeman who doesn't speak English as he's dishing out the huge on the spot fine!*

I've also had an A-frame come off whilst driving, miraculously with no damage to life or property. So personally, I now think they are darn right dangerous, and they scare me to bits! *More later!*

We will be covering the following topics throughout this book:

- Choosing the right caravan for your needs and circumstances
- New or second-hand?
- Matching the towing vehicle
- Weights, lengths and widths
- Loading
- Payloads
- Motor-movers
- Awnings
- Accessories to make things easier
- Storage
- Mirrors
- Towing
- Reversing
- Insurance
- Maintenance
- Wintering
- Selling
- Towing Abroad

Navigating this Book

If you have the digital PDF version of this book, you will be able to take advantage of the various hyper-links to other sites where applicable. You can also instantly revert to the contents page by clicking on the '$\leq$' icon, which is in the footer of every page, next to the page numbers. You can then click on any item in the contents section to get there immediately.

If you have the paper-back version, or any other digital version where the links don't work you can download the digital PDF version at no extra charge by using the link towards the end of the book.

Choosing the Right Caravan

Caravans come in a huge variety of designs, sizes, weights, lengths, widths and of course prices. Which will be right for you will depend on your circumstances and budget. Quite possibly you'll have a family, making a 3 / 4 berth van essential. Caravans are certainly great for family holidays and of course you can also take your furry friends with you as well. We never go anywhere without our cat!

In years gone by there were numerous UK manufacturers of vans, but gradually they have amalgamated or liquidated leaving us with the following:

- Eldiss
- Luna
- Coachman
- Bailey
- Swift (Eccles / Bessacarr / Sprite)
- Vanmaster
- Freedom
- Barefoot

And the folding campers:

- Riva (Dandy)
- Pennine (Conway)

All of these are certainly worth considering.

There are also many non-UK manufacturers which are perhaps also worth considering such as:

- Adria
- Burstner
- Hymer
- Eriba
- Rapido
- Tabbart
- Hobby
- LMC
- Knaus
- Wingamm
- Dethleff

Sadly, I have to state that *in the main,* the build quality of many of the European makes is better than many of the UK ones. That being said we chose a Bailey for our latest van due to the layout and other factors which I shall divulge as we progress.

The main disadvantages of the non-UK makes are:

- Insurance - *some companies won't insure them!*
- Higher theft rate - *allegedly*
- Pre-owned ones may not be CRIS registered
- Door on the opposite side - *no big deal!*
- Less dealers and aftercare establishments

- Much higher depreciation

- Most are ugly - *actually **all** are ugly (Eriba excepted)!*

But I can really see why the *'travelling community'* tend to prefer them - they're built to last!

New or Second-hand

In a nutshell, the more you pay for a caravan, the more you will ultimately lose, so getting it right will cut your losses to a great extent.

If buying a new van, you will have no choice but to go to a dealer but do remember that the price variation between different dealers for exactly the same thing can be vast - *there's always deals to be had!*

But it probably makes sense to buy pre-owned for a first van, mainly because it's doubtful that you really know what is absolutely right for you. And if you buy pre-owned sensibly, you may not lose anything at all when you come to sell.

If you decide to initially buy pre-owned, your next decision will be whether to buy from a dealer or privately.

Well, I'd certainly recommend going around all the dealers to see all the new designs and layouts as well as their selection of pre-owned vans. But don't take too much notice of their initial prices as in many cases they are pitched so that they can drastically reduce the price to let you have an *'amazing deal'* that's *still* overpriced!

When I buy second-hand cars, I find an example of what I'm looking for, get the reg number and pump it into *'webuyanycar.com'*, then at least I'll know what I would get for it easily if I decided to sell it again the next day. Through doing this I've minimised my losses on cars. In one case I even made a profit - *vary rare!*

With caravans it's a fair bit different as there is little way of knowing how many miles they've done or how much they've been kicked around other than by visual checks. But just the same as cars, there are guides showing the second-hand value of the various makes and models manly based on age and condition.

There are also companies for caravan purchases similar to *'webuyanycar.com'*, so if you contact one of them with details of what you want to buy under the pretext of selling it, you'll find out the bottom-line price. This is a good thing to do when you are genuinely selling as well - *see dedicated chapter further on.* But remember that this will be the *desperation* price and the difference between this price and the forecourt price will be vast.

The advantage of buying from a dealer is that you may have some sort of warranty and after care, but personally, I think the best deals are to be had privately. You can get a good idea of how well a van has been looked after by the property of the people who are selling it. A van previously owned by an old couple who have nurtured it, covered the seats and carpets, had it regularly serviced and kept it on their driveway can be an excellent buy and may be worth paying a little over the odds for. We've successfully bought several caravans and motorhomes privately, but you have to be careful.

Always, check service history, any existing warranties and very importantly *damp* issues - it's not a bad idea to get a damp meter.

Gumtree, eBay, Preloved, Facebook (Marketplace) and the private ads in all the various caravan magazines are good places to look, but also make sure you know the sort of price that you'd pay from a dealer (after they've reduced their initial crazy price).

Layouts

On the surface it seems that a suitable layout is the main factor, but there are many other factors which we'll be dealing with which could sway your decision.

Obviously, you'll need a layout that suits your individual requirements particularly regarding adequate sleeping facilities for your family *and animals if necessary.*

Some layouts have designated beds while others have daytime seating that converts. It could be said that designated beds are a waste of space, but for some they are an essential.

In the designated bed range, there are generally four options being:

- Twin singles (which can also be used as additional seating)

- French bed, where one side is against a wall - these can be great space savers, but the big downside is that one person has to jump over the other to use the loo in the middle of the night!

- Island bed, which is the most space greedy, but also certainly the most comfortable, where both occupants can egress without disturbing the other

- Bunk beds, either fixed or convertible - ideal for some

Beyond the sleeping arrangements, there are numerous kitchen and shower room designs and of course all available in varying qualities.

Following are diagrams showing some of the most popular layouts with daytime and night-time views. Most manufacturers do variants of these and more.

2 Berth - no fixed bed

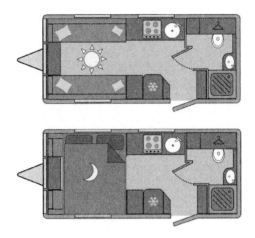

4 Berth with 'French' fixed bed

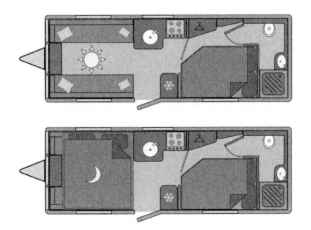

4 Berth with island fixed bed

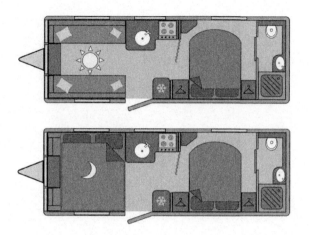

4 Berth with 2 single beds

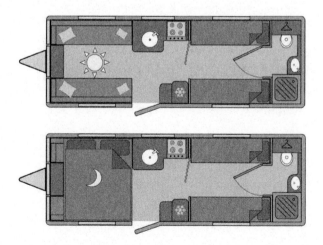

6 Berth with bunk beds

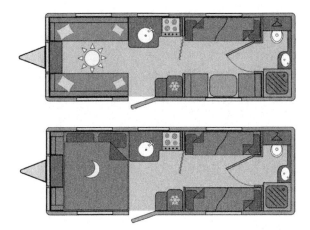

Curiously the larger vans are not a great deal more expensive than the smaller ones. But It's all too easy to get blown away by the spacious designs whilst ignoring other crucially important factors such as:

- Height

- Weight

- Width

- Length

- Tow Car and

- Licence Restrictions

We'll be dealing with these next along with other important factors.

Height

Most vans tend to be approximately 2.6m high - that's about 8' in old money *plus* whatever else you stick up there, like aerials, aircon units, solar panels etc.

Generally, it's quite rare that this height will be affected by low bridges or even *most* service stations, *but* you must always be aware as there are some restrictions, particularly toll booths, ferries and low trees on sites etc. - *especially in Spain!*

But regardless of height restrictions, the height will affect the aerodynamics. Many vans have sloping fronts making them a bit more aerodynamic, but at best this will only reduce the problem.

If you are not already aware of this, the aerodynamics will reduce the mpg and stability of the unit, particularly at speed and / or in windy conditions.

Eriba with Roof Down

Some vans like the Eriba's and Rapido's have pop-up roofs to reduce the towing height, which of course improves the mpg and stability. Also, the Riva and Pennine folding campers are much lower when being towed and as such are much easier, safer and more economical for a novice.

So yes, *height matters!*

Weight

It's quite possible to get a small van that is very heavy and a large one that is comparatively light. Although generally, the bigger the van the heavier it will be. But you must check this out before buying as you will need to match the van weight with your tow car (which we'll deal with shortly).

Many of the different makes and models of vans have different body constructions which can create huge weight variations. We chose the Bailey Unicorn as I was particularly impressed with their Alu-tech construction which is also *fairly* lightweight.

On every caravan, you will find two very important figures, on a plate usually on the nearside somewhere (but also in the specification details). These figures are:

- MIRO - mass in running order, which is the weight of the van without any additions. Sometimes included in this figure will be about 50kg to consider the leisure battery, gas bottle and water in the boiler etc., - but check with the manufacturers or dealers to confirm this - on older vans there may be no allowance

- MTPLM - maximum technically permissible mass, or MAM - maximum authorised mass, which is the maximum weight that your van is allowed to be, and includes all your clobber

The *'Payload'* is the MTPLM less MIRO.

As an example, if the MTPLM is 1500kg and the MIRO 1350kg then the Payload is 150kg. But remember that *everything* that you add will come off this figure. A typical motor-mover weighs 30kg which is a big hunk off your payload; then add TV, chairs, awning, clothes, food etc., and it soon adds up.

Unless you weigh absolutely everything individually as you pack and consider any additional fitted items, the only way to tell if your van is overweight is to go to a public weighbridge.

Exceeding the MTPLM is potentially dangerous and is also a serious offence which could result in a licence endorsement as well as a fine. I say *potentially dangerous* as in many cases it's possible to have the van re-plated with a higher MTPLM thereby increasing the payload. This is in fact what we have done with our current van which has effectively doubled the payload from 125kg to 250kg.

You might think that something physical is done to the van to have this extra payload, but no, just pay 30 quid and you get a new sticker for the side and the new weight registered in the logbook - *fascinating!* If this can be done why not do it for all of them as a matter of course? *But,* by having the increased payload, you must have this legally matched to your tow car and of course it may possibly affect your eligibility to tow due to any licence restrictions. In our case, it was well worth it particularly as half of the original payload was taken up with the motor-mover and the fixed wind-out Fiamma blind which we had fitted to the roof.

Ok, so is a heavier van more difficult to tow?

Well yes and no. If you have a well-matched towing vehicle, a good stabilizer and it is all within your licence restrictions, then you'd hardly notice it as long as it's loaded correctly. But nothing comes free - the heavier the van, the worse the mpg will be and the more difficult it will be to manoeuvre on site - with or without a motor-mover.

So yes, *weight does matter!*

Width

Years ago, when there was far, far less traffic on the roads, the maximum UK towing width permissible was 7'6", although most were no more than 7'. Now the maximum permitted width is 2.55m (8'4") and the norm is about 7'6".

Personally, I find this incredible as (with the exception of motorways), the roads haven't got any wider. In fact, when you consider all the additional parked cars, most roads have become considerably narrower!

You might think that this isn't a huge problem. Well on big wide roads with gradual corners it isn't but get down some narrow lanes in Cornwall and meet yourself coming the other way and you might change your mind!

Of course, wider vans have the potential for much more internal comfort which helps sell them to the wife but believe me every inch of width makes towing more difficult in tight situations.

For newbies, I would recommend 7'2" or 7'3" max - they are available, but at first glance they all look the same! The Pennine and Riva folding campers by the way are only 6'6" and the beautiful, retro Barefoot caravan (https://www.go-barefoot.co.uk) is only 6'3" wide making them a great choice for the inexperienced, but there are others.

So yes, *width can cause many problems!*

Length

Length, without doubt is the most crucial factor with regards to towing problems particularly when coupled with width and especially in tight situations. This is mainly due to the rear end *'swing'* which I'll make clear shortly.

The maximum length for a trailer towed by a vehicle weighing up to 3,500kg is 7 metres (22'11"). This length does not include the A-frame.

When considering buying, you need to always look at the *'shipping length'* which *includes* the A-frame.

Why?

Because this is the length that the ferry companies and recovery services will be interested in. The A-frame incidentally is usually about 1 metre.

The longest van we've owned was the Bailey Vigo at 7.37m (shipping length).

Now the rear end swing.

The following diagram shows three vans 2.2m wide with the following (approximate) shipping lengths:

- 7.2m

- 6.2m

- 5.2m

In every case they are swinging 20 degrees to the right starting one metre away from a brick wall.

Rear End Swing

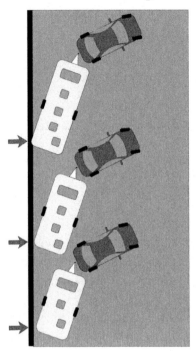

You'll notice that the longest van hits the wall causing extensive damage, the second one almost hits it but is probably totally unaware of the near miss, but the third one clears it easily, also probably totally unaware.

But most importantly, none of them can see the nearside rear in their mirrors, as this area is completely in their blind area (more of this shortly). They can all see the offside rear, but not the nearside!

This is frightening, I think I'll just stick to hotels and guest houses!

Well, the idea is not to frighten you, not too much anyway, it's just to make you aware. In actual practice this wouldn't be quite so bad as the whole lot would also be moving forward as it turns so it wouldn't actually be so extreme, but it's nevertheless something that you must always be aware of especially as you can't see it.

Of course, this problem becomes even worse on wider vans and less on narrower ones.

The most vulnerable times for this occurrence is obviously on narrow roads, often at or near your chosen caravan site. Wide roads with easy gentle corners are generally no problem. In extreme cases you may need to have your co-driver standing to the front nearside so that he / she can see both you and the nearside rear in order to guide you! We'll deal more with this problem shortly.

To assist your understanding of this problem, I strongly recommend that you buy a toy car and caravan to play with so that you see all this clearly. You can get these from most caravan dealers. I keep one in the van at all times and the wife thinks I'm mad!

Finally, some caravan sites won't accept vans over a certain length, often twin axles, and recovery can be a problem for any van over 7m shipping length.

So yes, *length matters big time!*

Tow car

For your safety, it's absolutely essential that your towing vehicle is correctly matched to your caravan. This is also a legal requirement.

The maximum legal weight that you are permitted to tow will be shown in your vehicle's registration document, but the maximum advisable limit is 85% of this figure. I personally have gone as high as 90% but I much prefer to stick to the 85% recommendations.

Ok, 85% of what?

It's 85% of the MTPLM as mentioned earlier.

Very often when I've been looking at vans in dealerships, the salespeople have tried to sell me vans right on the 100% limit and told me that it wouldn't be a problem - *well it wouldn't be to them would it?*

When I've confronted them with the 85% recommendations, I've more than once been informed that they'd never sell any vans if they stuck to those guidelines. Personally. I have absolutely no respect for dealers who act in this way, particularly to the inexperienced.

If you are inexperienced at towing, my advice is to start with a fairly small van (or folding camper) and stick rigidly to the 85% maximum limit. *And take a towing course!* So, with all this in mind, you have to either buy your van to match your car or buy a car to match the van that you want (which is what we usually do).

As a *general* guide, a 2-litre diesel is going to be about your minimum for a 4-berth van (but there are exceptions). Manual diesels are better for towing than petrol cars as there's less strain on the clutches due to the lower rpm and there's also more torque. For petrol cars, I would recommend automatics as they don't have clutches to burn out.

Our present and last previous towing car was / is a Ssangyong Korando 2 litre SE and 2.2 litre SE both of which towed our last two vans and present one very well. The first one which we bought new depreciated like a stone and the 5-year warranty covered absolutely everything that wasn't likely to go wrong but didn't cover anything that *did* go wrong! I was particularly miffed at a *'warped'* brake disc not being covered - worn out fair enough but warped? But having said this, I can't think of a more suitable reasonably priced vehicle for the job, which is why I bought the second one - *but this time pre-owned with a very low mileage!*

Yes, but we are being urged to dump diesels and go electric!

Well in the future this may well be the case, but at the time of writing this there are no *sensibly priced* electric cars suitable for towing, but I've no doubt that this will ultimately change.

You can easily check the suitability between your car and any caravan at http://towcar.info.

Towing Licence Restrictions

If you passed your car driving test on or after 1st January 1997 you can:

- Drive a car or van up to 3,500kg maximum authorised mass (MAM) towing a trailer of up to 750kg MAM

- Tow a trailer over 750kg MAM as long as the combined MAM of the trailer and towing vehicle is no more than 3,500kg

MAM is the limit on how much the vehicle can weigh when it's loaded.

You will have to pass the car and trailer driving test if you want to tow anything heavier.

If you passed your test before 1st January 1997 then you can:

- Drive vehicles between 3,500kg and 7,500kg carrying no more than 8 passengers plus driver with trailer up to 750kg (Cat. C1)

- Drive vehicles up to 3,500kg Maximum Authorised Mass (MAM) with up to 8 passenger seats and a driver with a trailer weighing up to 3,500kg (Cat. BE)

- Drive vehicles between 3,500kg and 7,500kg carrying no more than 8 passengers plus driver with trailer over 750kg, if combined vehicle and trailer weight isn't more than 8,250kg (Cat. C1+E).

When you reach 70 years of age you will lose the Cat. C1 for motorhomes over 3,500kg and C1+E unless you pay for and pass a medical, but you will still retain the Cat. BE for caravans - *this suits me fine!*

As an example, the MAM of our Korando is 2180kg and our present Bailey Unicorn Seville caravan is 1450kg (after re-plating) making a total of 3630kg. This would be over the limit had I not passed my driving test before 1997 and in fact would have been over by just 5kg had I not re-plated the van - *so you can see how important it is to check these figures!*

Storage

Having somewhere safe and secure to store your van when not in use is essential. We're fortunate in the fact that we have an area on our drive where we can keep our van virtually unseen behind locked gates which is ideal for security, loading, unloading and maintaining etc. As it's nice and handy, we also take all removable seats into the house in the winter to prevent them getting damp.

If you don't have place at your home you will need to find a CaSSOA storage to comply with most caravan insurance stipulations, but in some areas, much of the storage is full, so check this out before buying. See: http://www.cassoa.co.uk. If storing away from home, I recommend using some form of portable dehumidifier in the winter, either with crystals or rechargeable batteries.

CRIS Registration

All new caravans sold after 1992 in the UK should be CRIS registered which is basically the caravan version of a *'logbook'*. The registration shows the owner, previous owners, purchase date and VIN number of the vehicle. Older vans can also be registered.

If buying a second-hand van, unless it is very old, it would be unwise to buy it without the CRIS registration document. After purchase, the seller should sign the relevant part of the document which you need to send to CRIS with the appropriate fee to have the van registered in your name - similar to buying / selling cars.

If buying a second-hand van, you can also obtain a CRIS check to see if there is any outstanding finance or if the van has been an insurance write off, similar to an HPI check.

See: https://www.cris.co.uk/faqs

Maintenance

If towing a trailer or caravan on the road, it is your responsibility to ensure that it's roadworthy with regards to brakes, tyres, lights AND loading etc. Failure to do so could lead to prosecution.

Having your van serviced annually by a specialist is a pretty good idea. Normal caravan servicing will deal with the items mentioned above as well as the *'habitation'* items such as the internal gas, water and electrics etc.

Most vans have a manufacturer's warranty for one, two or three years but also a longer water ingress warranty. But if the van is not serviced annually according to their stipulations (usually by an NCC approved agent), the warranty will probably be null and void.

Summary

Whatever you choose you'll have to consider the following:

- Cost of purchase (new or second-hand)
- Warranty
- Depreciation and ultimately selling it
- Insurance
- Fuel costs (mpg)
- Ease of towing
- Storage, maintenance & servicing
- Ease of use (setting up etc.)
- Comfort level
- Driving licence restrictions
- Ferry costs (where applicable)
- Vehicle recovery
- Family requirements (including pets where necessary)
- The wife!

Our Caravans / Motorhomes

In this chapter I've listed *some* of the caravans that we have owned, why we bought them and why we sold them.

Apart from many years of caravanning with my parents as a child in the 50's and 60's our story begins in the 70's where we started off with a tent (due to not having much money).

We had several great years camping as a family with our frame tent and towed a small trailer for all the clobber which was no trouble to tow at all (even though it was unbraked). Also, in the 70's we bought a static van in the South of France and camped on the way there and back - *great times!*

Folding Campers 1980's

We've had two folding campers, the Pennine Pullman which we bought second-hand and the Dandy Destiny which we bought new. These are not to be confused with *'trailer tents'* although they are sometimes referred to as such. Both of these are fantastic for couples and families. We've toured extensively across France, Spain and the UK in both.

Depending on the weight of your towing vehicle, even the heaviest of these can be towed with a standard driving licence without taking an additional test.

Set up time is surprisingly quick - considerably less than a tent, and the level of comfort is comparable to a fairly large caravan.

Both of the models we owned came with a full awning (as an extra) which can be either set up for long stays or left off for short ones.

Each also has a double bed at each end as well as a dinette area which can be made into another double bed if required. Additionally, both have wardrobes, cooking hobs / grills, sinks, fridges, cassette toilets, heaters and leisure batteries. On top of all this they are lightweight and very easy to tow even with a 1300cc car and can be stored in the average garage. When we had the Pennine, I was short of space on our drive but managed to rent a secure council garage a few miles away!

Pennine Folding Camper

These are a truly brilliant alternative to a caravan or motorhome. If you can pick up one of these second-hand in good condition, you'll not regret it and would have a good chance of not losing any money when it comes to reselling as they are very much in demand.

One downside I can think of is that packing up in the rain can be tricky and in the case of the Pennine, after packing away in the wet, at some point it would be worth opening it up to dry out.

The Pennine sides and top are all canvas and can be erected by one person (although two makes it easier). The Dandy has hard sides and a soft PVC roof.

Not long before we sold our Dandy, we'd just about mastered the art of packing up in the rain without getting anything wet inside. The Dandy was surprisingly cool in hot weather as well as being warm in the cold.

Dandy (Riva) Destiny

My only grump (with both models) was that by the time we'd packed away and replaced the PVC cover my hands were filthy and the washroom was packed away inside - *could have used gloves I suppose, but I never thought of that!* Also, when stopping for a break in a lay-by, the toilet was unavailable - more of a problem for the wife than me! But having said that they can be erected fairly quickly without unhitching, *well it worked with our cars anyway!*

The only other downside I can think of is that like tents they are easy to break into.

Even though these are nowhere near as wide as the average caravan, you will still need a good set of extending towing mirrors.

Unless you have a monster of a car both of these can be towed on a standard UK driving license - but be sure to check weights and your driving license before buying one.

Smaller less refined versions are also available from both companies. See the Riva and Pennine websites for full details at:

- https://pennineoutdoorleisure.co.uk/folding-camper and

- http://www.rivadandysales.co.uk

Small Motorhome & Static 1990's

Well inevitably the kids grew up and moved on - but still give us plenty of grief - *the first 40 years of parenthood are the worst, then it starts to get a bit easier!* So, we bought our first motorhome which was a Swift Capri. This had a rear washroom, side kitchen, central dinette area which converted to a double bed and an additional double bed over the cab which we manly used for storage.

Swift Capri

As this was reasonably small there was no problem leaving sites to go shopping and off to restaurants etc., but I have to say it wasn't that spacious. But nevertheless, we toured the UK, France and Spain in this quite successfully.

Inevitably, we got fed up with this and bought a static van in Hornsea which we used for a couple of years. The depreciation on the Capri was very little.

Unsurprisingly, static vans are extremely spacious and comfortable. They're also expensive to buy, expensive to run and the depreciation is frightening. I think we had the static less than three years and lost about 50% of the purchase price. But at least we have the memories of having had a lovely van front line to the sea where we had many great times. But static vans don't do anything for the gipsy blood that must go through our veins.

Large Motorhome & Caravans 2000's

In 2003 I retired, and we moved to Cyprus. We had a lovely villa with all the trimmings, but I couldn't stand the summer heat, so in 2006 we sold up and moved back to the UK and bought a tag axle Hymer B74 motorhome accompanied initially by a car on a trailer. Having no fixed abode, we toured the UK for about six months then bought a bungalow in Louth (retaining the Hymer).

The car on the trailer turned out to be one hell of a pain (getting it on and off, plus the storage of the trailer on sites), so we got rid of it and bought a Smart car which we towed on an A-frame. We then toured France, Spain and Portugal for several months. Driving the Hymer was quite easy, but I did have a few height problems, mainly with trees on sites on Spain.

Another factor with the Hymer was that the weight was over 3.5 tonnes which was not a problem when we had it, but now that I've just reached 70 years of age, I would require a medical (that I would have to pay for).

Hymer B754

I've also noticed recently that there are an awful lot of new weight restrictions in France prohibiting vehicles over 3.5 tonne from many areas.

Needless to say, the Hymer was spacious and comfortable and it was a real privilege to have owned it. We sold it in 2010 after moving back to Sheffield. The running costs and depreciation on the Hymer were quite high, but part of this was due to the fact that we probably paid too much for it initially as we bought in a hurry after coming back from Cyprus - never a good idea!

We then decided to give up camping, but the bug didn't go away, so we bought a pre-owned Bailey Ranger caravan which we towed successfully with our Seat Altea.

Well, surprisingly the level of comfort in this almost matched the Hymer. It had a fixed 'French Bed' to the rear next to the washroom and a front dinette area.

Our Bailey Ranger

This van was reasonably easy to tow, as it was not too long, - *6.33m shipping length,* fairly lightweight and not as wide as many. I would say that this model (or similar) is an ideal first van for a small family with little or no towing experience. We toured extensively with this in the UK and France - a great little van that gave us no trouble whatsoever. We actually bought this on eBay for a fair price and when we came to sell, we didn't lose much at all.

The main downside with this van for us was the *'French Bed'* - no good for those with weak bladders! So, we decided that out next van must have either an island bed or two singles, but we had a cruise around the Norwegian fiords first - *nice!*

In 2014 we decided to move home again. Although we managed to sell our house ok in August, the one that we decided to buy was new and wasn't going to be ready until December. No problem! We bought another van and went off to Spain to keep warm.

This next van was a new Luna Ultima 554 which had the obligatory twin single beds. This was just a little longer, wider and heavier than the Bailey Ranger - *shipping length - 7.2m.* Although the Altea would have towed this legally, it would have meant going over the 85% weight guideline, so we thought we'd buy another more suitable towing vehicle. The Ssangyong Korando fitted the bill nicely and I have to say that they do tow well.

Our Lunar Ultima 554

Having never had any major problems with all our previous vans (new and second-hand) we weren't expecting any problems with this one either, but we were wrong, we had horrendous problems, mainly due to the flush leaking from the *superior* ceramic Dometic toilet which wrecked the floor and one of the walls, despite me being aware of the problem and moping it out several times a day. Luna ended up having it back for sixteen weeks to fix it and I wasn't at all impressed with their *'after care'* or the dealers.

The really worrying thing is that had we used the van as so many families do (a couple of weeks a year plus weekends), this problem wouldn't have come to light until the thing was out of warranty. But with us being away for five months in one go, it wasn't long before the problem became apparent.

Even though the problem was supposedly fixed, we didn't feel happy about keeping the Luna, so we traded it in for a new Bailey Unicorn Vigo.

When we traded the Luna in for the Bailey it (the Luna) was still under warranty, and the dealer who we bought both vans from went around it with a damp meter and found damp AFTER the manufacturers had supposedly fixed everything - not my problem anymore, but I just hope they fixed it properly before selling it on - *buyer beware!*

Apart from the problems, I have to say that the Luna was very comfortable, but I certainly would never buy another. Towing wise, with it being longer and heavier than the previous one, of course it was more difficult, mainly due to the increased swing. No trouble on the *'straight',* just the *'narrow'!*

Our Bailey Vigo and Ssangyong Car

We actually got a good *'end of season'* discount when we bought the Luna, so we did get a reasonable trade in price for it, which softened the blow on the depreciation.

The Bailey Unicorn Vigo was just a little longer, - *7.37m shipping length*, wider and heavier than the Luna and consequently more difficult to tow in restricted areas. The Korando still had no difficulty in pulling it *and stopping it!*

The main attraction with the Vigo was the island bed enabling easy in and out for both of us and the fact that it had a big fridge, which the wife wanted. Also, the general finish and build quality of the Unicorn range (although not perfect) was *much* superior to the Luna.

We toured France and Spain a couple of times with the Vigo, and yes it was very comfortable, but in my opinion a bit of a monster to tow, particularly for the distances that we travel. So due to my dislike of towing this, we decided to revert back to a motorhome and tow a car on an A-frame.

We found a very low mileage pre-owned Chausson Welcome with an island bed. Although the bed was very comfortable in this, the general comfort was not in the same league as the Bailey Vigo caravan. But nevertheless this was absolutely great to drive and gave us no problems at all, but we did have a major issue with the A-frame as briefly mentioned previously.

So, what exactly happened?

The A-frame attached via two anchorage bolts in the front of the car and one of them snapped as shown below.

Broken Anchorage Bolt on the Left

 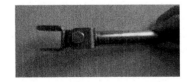

Fortunately we weren't travelling very fast, so I managed to stop almost instantly, which prevented the other bracket from also snapping with possible horrendous consequences.

As also briefly mentioned previously, the legalities of using A-frames abroad is highly dubious at best. So we decided to try a couple of trips without towing the car. To be quite honest they were pretty miserable. We had no problem with shopping as we'd stop at supermarkets *en-route* to stock up. Had we not had the cat with us, we could have used the Aires which are mainly situated in town centres, then we could have walked to restaurants etc. easily. But we needed to find rural sites which were suitable for our pussy to play happily and safely.

Our Chausson with Car on A-Frame

Had everything gone fine with the A-frame, we may well have kept the motorhome, but as this was not to be, we decided to go back to a car and caravan - but not a monster. I did consider a smart car on a trailer, but although we have plenty of room on our drive for a motorhome and car, we don't have the space for a trailer (even a small one is much bigger than you might imagine).

So, our latest set-up is a two berth Bailey Unicorn Seville which is shorter and lighter than our previous vans - *6.2m shipping length.* In fact, this was the shortest of all our recent vans, *but not the narrowest.*

Our Bailey Seville and Korando

Although there's been a lot of compromises, (the major one being that we no longer have a fixed bed), after getting used to it we are managing with this quite well. The wife still has her large fridge and I have the shorter length. We also have a Fiamma wind-out blind fitted to the roof which is a great asset and as this is above the awning rail, we still have the option to use an awning should we so wish. Basically, we've got the caravan rigged to be as close to a motorhome as possible, so that we can be set up quickly and easily with the minimum of hassle.

Essential Accessories

You could actually spend a fortune on caravan accessories, some are essential, some are useful, but many are a complete waste of money.

In this section is a list of the essential ones.

Leisure Battery

When buying from a dealer the leisure battery is rarely included, although probably will be if you buy privately. Some will require occasional topping up with distilled water, others will be sealed and require no maintenance.

If you have a motor-mover (which is a very good idea) then you will need one with a good Ah (amp hour) rating - 110 Ah is good.

When towing, your leisure battery will be charging from the towing vehicle's alternator and will also be charging when connected to an electric hook-up on site or via solar panels if fitted.

But if you are on a site without an electric hook-up remember that you might not have enough power left to use the motor-mover when the time comes to leave. This may or may not be a problem - depending on how you position the van!

Probably only a basic battery will be included in the manufacturers MIRO calculations, anything heavier will reduce your payload!

Gas Bottle

Again, if you buy new, the gas bottle and possibly the main gas pipe will *not* be included, but possibly will be on a pre-owned.

In the UK, there are two main gas types; *'butane'* and *'propane'*. The advantage of propane is that it has a lower freezing point; it's also lighter and burns hotter. The regulators between the two are not interchangeable, so you will need to make your choice and stick to it - *or buy another regulator.* We use propane as we often travel late in the year when butane may freeze.

Propane or Butane?

But whichever you use you will not be able to get your bottle refilled anywhere abroad as each country uses different bottles and regulators.

The only *'universal'* gas is *'Camping Gaz'* which you can buy refills for just about anywhere, but you can't connect them to your van without an adapter and / or alternative regulator - it's also *very* expensive.

Unless you use gas for heating, a normal full bottle should last you a very long time. Most modern caravans and motorhomes have electric and gas heating, so if you are connected to a hook-up it shouldn't be a problem.

If you intend camping regularly without an electric hook-up it might be worth your while buying an LPG tank and the connectors for all the countries that you intend travelling through - then you can fill up economically at most service stations.

Refillable LPG Gas Cylinders

Safefill   Alugas   Gaslow   Gasit

Another option that we once did when wintering in Spain is to buy a Spanish gas bottle and regulator. These are widely available second hand on most large camp sites in Southern Spain - look at the notice boards. You can also buy all the necessary connectors in the UK.

When we bought one of these in Spain a few years ago (2008). The going rate was about €10 for the empty bottle and €10 for the regulator.

Smoke / Gas Alarm

Most new vans now include smoke and gas alarms as standard. If you buy an older van where they are not included, you'd be wise to get them!

Electric cable

A mains hook-up cable is normally included with new caravans, but not necessarily with a second-hand one, but if you intend using electric hook-ups one of these is essential. We have two, a long one and a short one. Wherever possible I use the short one but occasionally I need both.

It's also a good idea to have a two-pin adapter and polarity checker if travelling abroad. We also have an adapter to connect to our mains at home.

Freshwater Carriers & Connectors

Unless you have an on-board water tank, which is very rare on UK caravans, you will need a freshwater container. We've had every type of water bottle going. The favourites seem to be the aqua-roll type, but I found these more of a space nuisance, so we went back to two 10 litre bottles which we wash out and sterilise on a regular basis - *works for us!* But having said that we never use the shower in the van and wherever possible use the site dish-washing facilities.

It's also a good idea to have a selection of pipes and connectors to fit all of the various sized taps, especially if you have large water carriers.

Wastewater Container

You can buy enormous roll along wastewater containers which take up stacks of room, we just use the smallest available to conserve space. The pipe connections are normally supplied with new vans, but not necessarily with used ones.

Mirrors

As your van or folding camper will be wider than your towing vehicle you will need mirror extensions for both offside and nearside. Towing without these would be nothing short of madness.

There are numerous types on the market, but apart from the various designs, the two main types are *flat* or *convex*.

The flat glass will give a true image, whereas the convex glass will give a wider range of view, but the images will appear further away than they actually are, which is ok as long as you are aware of this.

Some manufacturers recommend that you should use flat to the offside and convex to the nearside, but personally I prefer convex both sides. I suggest that you experiment with both and use whichever you feel most comfortable with.

Because they are so important, it's also a good idea to carry spares. I carry three spares. *I once had mine stolen on a ferry!*

Suction Mirror

I use a suction one on the nearside and a clamp on one on the offside.

Why?

Because I can then adjust both mirrors easily myself from the driving seat - the nearside suction one using the electric mirror mechanism and the offside one manually. The downside with the suction ones is that they are perhaps a little small.

Don't they drop off?

Mine never have, but they do have an elastic chord just in case.

But even with mirror extensions it must be noted that your zone of vision is still greatly reduced especially when turning and of course when reversing - *more of this later!*

Spare Wheel and Jack

It's not a legal requirement that you carry a spare wheel, jack and wheel brace, but it's got to be a good idea. On some new vans these are included as standard, on others they are an extra. It's also worth knowing exactly where to place the jack *before* you actually need it!

Wheel Chocks

Anytime you pitch or un-hitch on an incline, even with the van brakes on and the legs down, it's still a very good idea to chock the wheels.

I don't think I can remember a trip when I've not used my wheel chocks.

I've never known these to be given freely with new or second-hand vans, so this is one item that you will need to buy from the accessory shop.

Security Items

Security items are not essential unless you want to protect your investment and insure your van, in which case there will always be stipulations.

Most insurance companies stipulate that you at least use a hitch-lock and wheel lock when on sites and when the vehicle is at home or in storage. We have a Milenco hitch lock and an Alko axle wheel lock.

Milenco Hitch Lock

Other items are an alarm and tracker. Having one or both of these may reduce your insurance premium *slightly* but if you fail to activate them and then try and make a claim it could be tricky. We have both of these but have chosen not to declare them to the insurance company, so then there's no argument.

Note also that if you park up at a service area and leave the van, this is probably where it's most vulnerable. Few hitch-locks can be attached while the unit is hitched up. So, in this event I would advise using the wheel clamp (and alarm if fitted) even if it's only for a few minutes. Your van could be stolen and over a hundred miles away before you've even missed it!

As a further security measure, all new vans also have the windows etched in accordance with the CRIS guidelines.

Satnav for Caravans

Ok, maybe it's not *'essential'*, but it's certainly a very good idea!

No doubt you already have a satnav, but when towing a caravan or driving a large motorhome you really need one that takes the length, width and weight of your unit into account.

Several are available including:

- TomTom - https://www.tomtom.com
- Snooper - https://aguriworld.co.uk
- Aguri - http://www.snooper.co.uk

Also, some of the free mobile phone apps are coming along in leaps and bounds, so they too may be worth a look.

Up until recently we had a TomTom for caravans which was ok until it gave up the ghost. We've recently changed to an Aguri, which seems reasonable so far. Advantages of the Aguri are that it has an integrated dashcam (with SD card included), as well as many caravan sites *'built in'*. It's also an Android tablet! These come in two sizes with either 7" or a 5" screen. Well the wife insisted on a *big one,* but actually the small one would have been more appropriate for a car - *but what do I know?*

Map

Whatever type of satnav you have, don't go without a map as there's certain things that satnavs can't cope with, like diversions etc. and of course, you never know when your satnav will decide to self-destruct. Our TomTom died just after one of our trips abroad.

Entry step

We use a fairly lightweight double collapsible step which we're very happy with, but there are lots of different types to choose from.

Tyre pressure gauge

This is an essential low-cost item. Thankfully I've never experienced a blow out or puncture when towing a caravan. Although checking tyre pressures regularly won't necessarily eliminate this risk, it will help.

We also have a *'Tyrepal'* tyre pressure monitoring system which wirelessly constantly shows the vans tyre pressures and temperatures when driving along and sends out a warning if either reading becomes abnormal. I have to say that I am totally impressed with this device. See: https://www.tyrepal.co.uk .

Fire extinguisher

Carrying a fire extinguisher is compulsory in several countries, but it has to be a good idea in a caravan, especially when you start cooking. But do make sure that it's somewhere accessible. We also have a *'fire blanket'*.

Basic Tool Kit

At some point it's inevitable that you will need to do some sort of minor repairs or maintenance to your van when away, so a basic tool kit with at least the following items is advised:

- Hammer and mallet
- Torch with spare batteries
- Selection of screw drivers and spanners
- Pliers with wire cutters
- Insulation tape & Duct tape
- WD40

You'd be amazed at how many times I've met campers who've arrived at sites without a hammer!

Spare Bulbs

Make sure you have spare bulbs and fuses for your car and van and the tools to fit them, which is a legal requirement in many countries.

When we had the Smart Car, I had a head-light bulb blow and decided I was going to change it in a few minutes before going shopping; but when I looked at the handbook it said: *'go to main agent'!*

I then found out how to do it via the internet and it took me a day. Now that I know how to do it, I could probably do it in half a day - but even so how mad is that? To be fair, I think they've improved this on more recent models.

Toilet Blue and Pink Flush

Regardless of what you intend doing in your toilet you'll need some *'blue'* for the cassette and *'pink'* for the flush. You only need a very small amount of this stuff as it's extremely strong so don't overdo it!

There is also a *'green'* alternative which is suitable for septic tanks.

First Aid Kit

In many countries carrying a First Aid kit is a legal requirement, it's also quite sensible!

Number Plate

Well, this sounds pretty obvious, but actually when we bought the last van, the dealer never mentioned it, but fortunately I'd already ordered one from eBay. In the UK you will need a yellow rear plate with the same letters / numbers as your towing vehicle. In most cases these are fixed using double sided sticky tape - *so no drilling necessary!*

Warning Triangle & Reflective Yellow Vest

Carrying a warning triangle and immediately accessible reflective jackets or vests for all occupants is compulsory in many countries in the event of a breakdown or accident and is certainly a good idea. Two triangles are required in Spain.

Spare Glasses

If you wear glasses, in many countries carrying a spare set is a legal requirement. It's also a pretty good idea!

International Driving Licence

Check whether or not you need an international driving licence if travelling abroad and note that there are different ones for different countries. In the UK these are available from most post offices on production of your UK licence, identity photo and fee.

Green Card Insurance

When travelling in some countries you may need a green card insurance for both your car AND your caravan. Check with your insurance company before travelling. Years ago, they used to be green and printed on card. *Now they are neither!*

GB Plate / Sticker

If travelling abroad, you will need an *International Registration Letter* or *International Circulation Mark* both on your towing vehicle and caravan showing the country where the towing vehicle is registered. Obviously in the UK this will be a **'GB'** plate or sticker.

These are available for pennies on eBay but will cost you considerably more on the ferry if you forget!

Worthwhile Accessories

This section shows the accessories that are not necessarily essential but will often make life easier or more pleasurable. But before buying anything always consider how it will affect your payload and storage.

Motor-movers

There are two main types of motor-movers available; the *'bigfoot'* type which temporarily replaces the jockey wheel and the type that permanently attach to the van. I've had both!

The *'bigfoot'* type is ideal if you need it just for manoeuvring at home. We used one of these with the Dandy folding camper as I had a problem reversing through our gate and down a steep drive, but for general use on sites etc., the Dandy wasn't a problem, so the *'big foot'* was left at home in the garage.

The type that fit onto the vans are by far the most common and a good proportion of caravanners now have them, basically because we are a lazy useless bunch. My father would have been totally appalled, as he could reverse anything anywhere, but unfortunately, I can't - *sorry Dad!*

In order to operate them you will need to clamp the mover to the wheel usually with a wheel brace, then turn the unit on via a specific plug-in switch, then turn the remote on, release the van brakes and off you go. But be careful, you can do a lot of damage quickly with these things. To date the only dent I've ever put in a caravan was with one of these on our gate post!

After use, be sure to re-apply the handbrake and turn the remote off BEFORE releasing the mover from the wheels especially if you are on a gradient - otherwise it could go rolling off on its own!

Motor-mover

 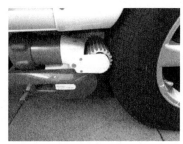

Ideally you will also need a 110Ah leisure battery to operate one of these.

The only negative with these is that they are quite heavy (about 30kg) and this will reduce your payload considerably, but for me they are an essential that I could never do without - *sorry again Dad!*

ATC

ATC stands for Automatic Trailer Control. It's an electronic anti-snaking system for touring caravans. Some vans such as our Bailey Unicorn have ATC fitted as standard but no doubt this can be fitted as an extra to most vans if required. ATC is particularly advantageous in windy conditions and / or when overtaking or being overtaken by lorries on motorways etc.

I've towed thousands of miles both with and without ATC and have to say that although it's only kicked in for me occasionally, I can really feel it when it does. Any and every device that makes towing safer has to be good!

Many insurance companies including Caravan Guard offer a discount when this and other safety and security items are fitted.

Awnings

There's no doubt that an awning can be a great asset to your caravan. There are several different types to choose from such as:

- Full length awning
- Porch awning (enclosed) - various sizes
- Inflatable porch awning
- Canopy with sides only (no front)
- Canopy without sides
- Awning in a bag (with or without sides)
- Fiamma / Omnistor fixed wind-out blind

How you intend using them will determine which one is most suitable or you. We've had all of them.

A full awning will literally double your space, but they can be quite heavy on your payload and also come in the same category as frame tents from the erection point of view - *divorce material!* In my opinion, these are great if you have a family and / or you are staying at a single destination for a fair while - but not ideal for erecting when touring.

I would say that a porch awning is a pretty good compromise, as if you choose the right one, they can be put up *fairly* quickly and easily and are less of a pull on your payload. These will give you shelter for cooking outside without too much hassle.

Our Porch Awning on the Luna

When we had the Luna and Vigo caravans, we often took the above porch awning and also a simple canopy with sides but no front, which gave protection from the odd shower and also *'bombing birds'!*

Also ideal for touring, are the canopies without sides which are even quicker and easier to erect and fold up to a fairly small square. Isabella do one with lightweight glass fibre poles - slide on, two or three vertical poles, peg out and its up - brilliant, and low cost!

The awning in a bag is another more expensive option. These slide onto the awning rail and stay put while you are driving, then simply unroll, slide the legs out of the roll and peg out. Optional sides and fronts are also available for these. The disadvantage is that they will add a couple of inches to your nearside (UK) high level width.

The flavour of the month seems to be the inflatable type. Well in a fit of madness we bought one of these and sold it after one test run. These are expensive, very heavy, bulky, not that quick to erect and in my opinion totally overrated. And had the cat started pole dancing round it with her claws, it would have ended up in the bin!

Finally, the fixed Fiamma or Omnistor wind out sun-blinds as seen on most motorhomes. These are fairly expensive and a huge pull on your payload. Without doubt these are the quickest and easiest to use - just wind it out, peg it down if you want to and your sorted!

We have one of these on our current van fitted to the roof, so there's no overhang, and as it's above the awning rail we still have the option to use a standard awning instead. The greatest advantage is that even if stopping for one night, it still gets used, whereas the other types can be just too much hassle.

Ours cost just under £1000 fitted by CB caravan servicing in Huddersfield - http://cbcaravanservicing.co.uk who I have to say I was most impressed with - *a true professional who really knows what he's doing!*

Our Fiamma Wind-out Blind

In all cases, you will need a selection of good quality pegs for various terrains and a storm strap. Wherever possible I use pegs that I can screw in with my electric drill!

Groundsheet

Whether you use an awning, canopy or neither you will most likely find an entry groundsheet very useful to help reduce the amount of mud, sand, grass or dust etc. that gets into your van.

Even if stopping for one night in most cases this is the first thing we put down. Depending on the ground, we use plastic groundsheet pegs or 4" nails with washers.

Barbeques

Of course you want a barbeque, you're on holiday, but you need to think about size and weight as well as carrying the fuel.

We've had all the expensive gas ones that take up stacks of room but have given them the heave-ho years ago!

Our latest barbecue is a portable fan assisted one. I suppose it's a little bulky being about a cubic foot, but I have to say that it works incredibly well - being quick, easy to clean, uses hardly any fuel and comes complete with a carrying bag.

This cost just under £40 on eBay.

Berndes Fan Assisted Barbecue

Air Conditioning

If you intend going to hot places during the summer an aircon unit will save you from roasting. But they are one heck of a pull on your payload. In fact, with most payloads, if you have a motor-mover, wind-out blind and aircon, there won't be much payload left for much else unless you also upgrade the plating!

The best place to have an aircon unit is on the roof, but always have anything on your roof fitted by a professional who should seal it correctly to avoid water ingress.

Some aircon units also have a blown air heater incorporated which is very handy if your van has only gas heating.

We've had aircon in the past, but for us it's not an issue as there's no way that we are going anywhere hot in the summer months.

Alternatives are roof fans or portable air-coolers which are much lighter.

Drill leg winder

Next to the motor-mover, the leg winder attachment for a battery-operated drill has to be my most important extra. When arriving on sites, our legs can be down in seconds with no effort, but don't forget to charge your drill and always keep the manual winder as a back-up!

And what do they cost?

Next to nothing - get one!

Spirit level

Unless you're not bothered about your blood running to your head at night, you'll need to get level and will consequently need a small spirit level. Get level side-ways first with a ramp on one wheel if necessary and then raise / lower the jockey wheel to get the level front to rear!

Getting level with a caravan is actually a fair bit easier than with a motor-home due to using the jockey wheel.

Ramps

I bought a set of ramps when we had the motorhome, which we then needed regularly. But as caravans are much easier to get level, if you need a ramp it will only be on one side. These are worthwhile but perhaps not essential.

Leg pads

Another really worthwhile accessory. Instead of pratting about with blocks of wood under the legs, these just clip on and stay there. But the yellow top-quality ones are best.

Wellies & Poncho

Sod's law states that at least some of the time you will arrive at your destination in the pouring rain, so being prepared with wellies and a waterproof poncho will save a degree of pain. And don't think that they won't be necessary in the summer in France or Spain etc., I've needed them more there than in the UK!

Reversing Camera

Not essential, as you may think that you will never have to reverse. Well, believe me there will be times when you'll need to reverse and without a reversing camera, you will obviously need to rely on someone else to guide you.

A reversing camera can also double up as a *'mirror'* as long as it's activated by a switch rather than being automatically engaged when selecting reverse gear.

Solar panels

Some vans (our Bailey Unicorn being one of them) have solar panels fitted as standard. Although generally not essential, personally I think they are great. We also have them on our house which effectively makes our energy bills nil - *they're probably frazzling my brains, but I haven't noticed anything so far!*

These of course can dispense with the need for electric hook-ups to a certain extent. But do remember that if you are relying on your motor-mover at the end of your stay, there might not be enough power left!

There are also free-standing solar panels available but be careful how you connect them.

Spare Keys

You'd be wise to keep a note of all your key numbers and always carry at least one spare! If you have an Alko wheel lock, make sure you register it with them otherwise you'll never get a replacement key if you need it!

Inverters

Large and small inverters are available enabling you to run 240v appliances from your leisure battery. Obviously the bigger the inverter, the sooner you will ultimately flatten your battery. I would suggest that they are only suitable if you have a solar panel.

We just have a couple of the 150w inverters which are very low cost but enable us to use a 240v TV and satellite box without mains hook-up - *useful when waiting at ferry ports!*

Vacuum Flask

A vacuum flask with boiling water can save a lot of time when stopping for a refreshment break or waiting for a ferry. I wouldn't recommend actually making tea in it, as it goes all sort of grey. Just fill it with boiling water and brew up when you're ready. Yes, I know you can't make a proper brew without the water being *actually* boiling, but it does work to a reasonable extent and saves a lot of time.

Safe

Thankfully, we've never had problems with sneak thieves or worse etc., but I guess that a correctly fitted safe can be useful. *If you get a tradesman to fit one, make sure you kill him afterwards so that no-one knows where it is!*

We just tend to split cash and credit cards up and hide it in different locations - but not the bottom of the wardrobe which is the first place they'll look. The only trouble is that sometimes we forget where we've hidden it, but it's also sometimes a nice surprise later to find a few hundred quid that we'd forgotten about!

Carpet runners

If you intend using your van as we do, for fairly long trips, this can put a lot of wear on your carpets. With this in mind, we leave the original carpets at home and use low cost carpet runners instead. We also use seat covers and different cushions so that when we finally sell the van, all the originals will still be pristine.

Front Caravan Cover

Whilst I'm not a fan of the full caravan covers except in certain circumstances, I think the front covers which can be used whilst towing are an excellent idea and will save having to wash off all the dead flies, grime and tar from the front of your van.

The only reason that we don't use one of these is because Kizzie (the cat) travels in the van and likes to look out of the front windows. I also like to keep an eye on her in my mirror.

Cool box

Unless you have a large fridge as we have in our Unicorn Seville, you will more than likely need to supplement your existing fridge with a cool box, particularly if travelling abroad for a while. Make sure you get one that is 12v *and* 240v.

When towing caravans with smaller fridges, we generally kept one in the car while travelling and then just left it plugged in outside of the van when on site as they can be quite space invasive, but probably worth it.

Bedding

Sleeping bags with removable washable inner liners are ideal for most types of camping. Duvalay do a good selection, but there are others.

We just use normal sheets and duvets. We take both lightweight and heavy quilts for varying temperatures and a change of sheets and covers.

Snow Chains

I've never been in the position where I've needed snow chains with or without a van, but if returning from Spain in the winter, you may well need them and on some routes, they are compulsory. But perhaps a better option is to use winter tyres. The safest and easiest routes across the Pyrenees is the South side via Figueres (A9 /E15) or the North side St Jean de Luz - San Sebastian (E5). But to be honest I would avoid towing in the snow unless you are very experienced.

Sog Toilet

If you plan on going wild camping and intend *'screaming'* at your toilet, a *'Sog'* toilet can be a great asset. These are basically a carbon filter to reduce smells and eliminate the need for *'blue'* and are easily fitted to your cassette door with a pipe that goes into the cassette.

We used one when we lived in the Hymer and I can confirm that they do work. But if you only intend using your toilet for *'whispering'* as we do now, then they're not really worth the trouble of fitting.

Clothes Lines & Pegs

If you intend travelling for a while as we do, you will probably need to do at least some washing unless you're a total scumbag!

We use a portable carrousel which doubles as the satellite dish tripod!

Outside Table & Chairs

Always choose lightweight aluminium in order to preserve your payload. And for packing, the ones that fold flattest are best. *'La Fuma'* do some good ones that double as both relaxing and eating chairs. In many caravans, your inside table can also be used outside which is great, if not, again go for lightweight and easy packing away. Actually, we leave the inside table at home and carry a couple of outside aluminium ones.

Foot Pump and Puncture Repair

Not essential but very worthwhile. I've gone years without ever having a puncture, but three times have had *three* punctures in a day - *bad days!* As a result of these unlikely occurrences, I've learnt to carry a few cans of *tyreweld* or similar to get me out of trouble but note that this stuff is only very temporary.

Suction Hooks

I find it infuriating that nearly all camp site showers provide insufficient hooks. What does a hook cost for goodness sake? This problem can be solved easily by carrying a few suction hooks which cost virtually nothing. But don't forget to remove them from the wall afterwards - you probably will forget, so it's worth having a few!

Outside / Awning Cooking Items

In good weather, it's far better to do all or most of your cooking outside as apart from anything else this will save wear and tear on your van.

A lightweight fold up aluminium camp kitchen can be very useful, especially with a splash guard to save getting grease on the side of your van.

If you use electric hook-ups taking a *low wattage* induction hob, kettle, grill, microwave and toaster will save your valuable gas supply. But you can rarely use more than one of these appliances at a time particularly abroad. The amperage available at ACSI campsites is always shown in their details. Some Spanish ones are as low as 3 amps, but most are 6 amps or more.

Satellite TV

Just about all caravans now come with a factory fitted TV aerial which for most UK usage is fine. However, there are areas in the UK where reception is poor or non-existent, parts of the East Yorkshire coast being one of them. So, for these areas or if you intend venturing abroad, a satellite dish may be a good option.

As well as the dish (and tripod) you will also need a *'Freesat'* or *'Sky'* reception box or the facility within the TV, a compass and the ability to set it all up. I've seen people pratt about with these for hours and get nowhere, but it's simple. To get Astra 2 (for all UK channels) the dish needs to be pointing more or less to 145° S.E. The upward angle at which the dish should be pointing depends on the area, but I've never failed to get it with just a little trial and error. If you can't get it fairly quickly, check all the connections and make sure that the dish is not pointing at a wall or tree in which case you'd be wasting your time.

We use a small *'Multimo'* dish which has an incredible reception for its size. I mount this on a tripod which is also used for drying washing at the same time. I wouldn't change this.

There are many more expensive self-seeking versions on the market which I have considered but concluded that for me they're just not worth it as they are only any use in the UK areas of bad reception and North to Mid France. I've found that I can't get Astra 2 much further South than Limoges. Beyond there and as far South as the Costa Dorada you can get Astra 1 which will give you Sky News and a few other channels that you wouldn't want to watch unless you are totally sad and desperate.

Satellite dishes can also be very space greedy although not heavy, which is why many motorhomes have them fixed on the roof. The downside to having them fixed on the roof is that if you happen to park up just in the wrong place, you won't get a signal without moving the van. Also, they are far more effected by wind up there and could cause damage if you forget to put them down.

When we go to Spain in the winter months, we take a recordable *'digi'* box with us with a stack of films that we record earlier in the year.

At quite a few of the sites in the Benidorm area and further down you can get a satellite cable connection for a small consideration which is great for anyone *'wintering'* or *'full timing'* in Spain.

Internet

Internet is available at many camp sites home and abroad, if you're lucky it will be free, but some charge astronomical fees.

For me this is no problem as I use my own mifi (about £30 on eBay) with a *'3'* or *'Vodafone'* sim card. There are various short-term deals available. Which will be best for you will be determined by the length of your trips. Sometimes we have a short-term contract (which can be cancelled with 30 days' notice) and sometimes we buy a *'pay as you go'* sim which lasts for a year but doesn't include a huge amount of usage.

3 Mifi

See:

- http://www.three.co.uk/Store/Mobile_Broadband and
- https://www.vodafone.co.uk

Of course, I always take advantage of any free connections that are available, thereby preserving my allowance. You also need to adjust your PC to a *'metered'* connection to stop it from downloading unnecessary rubbish when it feels like it.

Another way of getting free internet abroad is via *'Fon'* hotspots. Fon is a Spanish company, but curiously there are many more Fon Hotspots in France and the UK than in Spain. In order to be eligible to access these hotspots, you need to either use BT for your internet in the UK (which I don't) or have a Fon router attached to your home network and thereby create a hotspot for others to use - a brilliant idea all about *'sharing'!*

And finally, just like in the UK there are free open hotspots at most restaurants abroad including MacDonald's etc.

Well beyond all this lot, there's a whole host of expensive useless items out there, all of which add weight and space, so think carefully before you buy.

Towing

Now to the *'nitty gritty'!* This chapter will cover the following points:

- Loading your van
- Tyres
- Coupling up
- Pre-drive check list
- Un-coupling
- Mirrors and zones of vision
- Moving off and accelerating
- Braking
- Speed limits
- Snaking
- Crosswinds
- Overtaking
- Turning corners
- Motorways
- Reversing
- Plan your routes
- Setting up at your destination

Loading Your Van

All caravans are designed so that they are correctly balanced when empty, allowing a bit more weight at the front end to achieve an acceptable *'nose weight'*. When packing ensure that any heavy items are placed more or less on the axle, then equal amounts of lighter items front and rear. Avoid anything heavy in top cupboards, save these for towels, clothes and melamine crockery etc. Then make sure that all cupboards are closed securely. Keep all your saucepans and tins of beans in the lower cupboards.

You can check the nose weight of the van by using bathroom scales and a short broom handle or by purchasing a device specific for this purpose.

Make no mistake about it, incorrect loading can be dangerous as it is a major contributing factor to *'snaking'* which can often lead to disaster.

Tyres

It shouldn't need mentioning how important correct tyre depths and pressures are, but when towing this is certainly more important both on the van and the towing vehicle. If your tread depth is getting anywhere near the legal limit before a long towing trip it would be advisable to change them earlier rather than later.

But it must be noted that whereas car tyres generally need changing as a result of tread wear, caravan tyres often need changing as a result of the rubber perishing due to age and sunlight etc. With this in mind it is advised that caravan tyres are changed (or at least inspected by an expert) every five years regardless of the tread depth.

Additionally, covering the tyres from direct sunlight in very hot places is also advisable.

As mentioned previously, we have a *'Tyrepal'* tyre pressure monitoring system which constantly shows the van's tyre pressures and temperature. In certain circumstances this device could be a life saver! A blow out at speed could kill you in any vehicle, *but it could kill you twice when towing!*

Coupling Up

If you've never hitched a van before, please ***do not*** rely on this information alone. It's not difficult, but you are advised to get someone who does it regularly to show you in practice - all dealers will do this! Even if you have done this before, remember that new equipment may be different to what you are used to. The implications of getting this wrong don't bear worth thinking about!

On the most common Alko stabilizer hitches there are two levers. The top lever locks / unlocks the stabilizer. The second lever which is underneath the first, locks the hitch to the tow-ball.

Procedure for coupling with an Alko Stabilizer:

- Ideally hitch-up on the level or as close to level as possible, at least until you know what you are doing

- Raise the jockey wheel so that the hitch on the van is higher than the tow-ball on the car

- Reverse the car so that the tow-ball is under the hitch - you will need someone to guide you; or bring the van to the car using the motor-mover

- Apply the brakes on both the van and car - also leave the car in first gear (with the engine switched off)

- If the motor-mover has been used, disconnect it and turn it off at the main switch

- Raise the stabilizer lever to access the hitch lever

Stabilizer Lever Raised Revealing Hitch Lever

- Slowly lower the jockey wheel to allow the hitch to lock on to the tow-ball. You may need to raise the hitch lever and possibly release the van brakes (slowly) to get the van positioned correctly

- As the hitch locks into position, the hitch lever will drop closed and the indicator button will show green

- If all is correct push down the stabilizer lever to lock the stabilizer in position

- Double check that the hitch lever is closed and that all is secure

- If all is correct, retract the jockey wheel ensuring that the inner and outer tubes are slotted into the appropriate slots, then loosen the clamp on the A-frame and raise the jockey wheel to the highest position for towing and re-tighten the clamp. Make sure the clamp and jockey wheel spindle are both fairly tight so that they don't come undone when towing

Jockey Wheel in various positions

- Attach the breakaway cable to the attachment point on the tow-bar. The breakaway cable is designed to apply the van brakes in the event of the unit becoming un-coupled whilst moving

- Connect the 12-volt electrics. Most vans built around 2008 or later will have the 13-pin twist sockets. If your tow car has the 7-pin socket, you will need an adapter. The electrics work your caravan lights, fridge, ATC if fitted as well as charge your leisure battery. If you have difficulty connecting the twist socket, the alignment may need re-setting; there is a small tool available for this purpose - make sure you have one. If your van has

ATC, the green light will illuminate to confirm that it's working (you may need to turn on the car's ignition to see this)

- Get your partner to assist with checking the caravan lights (side, brake, fog and indicators)

- Have a final check before moving off

- After moving off, if it doesn't feel right, stop and check

Additionally, **DO NOT** grease your cars tow-ball if using an Alko stabilizer hitch, as the stabilizer relies on friction. This would be about as stupid as oiling your brake pads! If your tow-ball has previously been greased, remove all traces of it before using it and if you have hitched up with a greased ball, you will probably need to replace the stabiliser pads.

Also be aware that the friction pads are a service item and will need replacing when worn or contaminated. Anyone is capable of changing these, it's very simple and there are several YouTube videos with clear explanations.

Inside Hitch – Showing pads left and right

Pre-Drive Check List

When just leaving home or a site is actually one of your most vulnerable times. As well as having a check list for all the things you don't want to forget, it's also a good idea to have a pre-drive check list as follows:

- Load the van evenly and secure all heavy or glass items
- Check all internal cupboards and lockers are closed and secure
- All skylights and windows closed and secure
- External lockers and entry door closed and locked
- Gas off
- Fridge to 12v
- All legs wound up correctly
- Check nose weight
- Towing car secure - handbrake applied and in gear before hitching
- Caravan securely hooked onto car - green button showing
- Alko stabiliser tightened - where applicable
- Safety cable attached
- Electrics connected and lights checked
- ATC light correct - where applicable

- Motor-mover switched off and disconnected from wheels

- Jockey wheel fully retracted up and secure

- Van brakes released - gently

- Tow car mirrors attached and adjusted

- If leaving a site, check ground for left-behinds especially pads, ramps, chocks and pegs that will give you or someone else a puncture and / or bugger the lawn mower

- Drive off slowly - stop immediately if it doesn't feel right

It's not a bad idea to print off this list or similar, laminate it and keep it in your car. It's so easy to forget something important.

Un-Coupling

When reaching your destination, if possible un-couple on the level. If you have to un-couple on a gradient choose downhill if you have the choice. If you are forced to un-couple uphill be aware that if the nose weight is light the front of the van may fly up whilst un-hitching. If you have reason to believe that this may occur, wind one or both of the rear legs down about 75%.

To un-couple proceed as follows:

- Apply handbrake on tow car, switch off engine and engage first or reverse gear

- Apply brake on caravan and chock the van wheels if on a steep gradient

- Remove the 12v electric cable

- Remove the breakaway cable

- Loosen the jockey wheel clamp, lower it to the ground and re-tighten the clamp

- Release the Alko stabilizer lever (top lever)

- Wind the jockey wheel up slowly and at the same time raise the hitch (lower) lever

- Very shortly the unit will become un-hitched

- Raise the jockey wheel enough so that the hitch is completely clear of the tow ball

- Manoeuvre the van into your chosen position, get level and wind down the legs before entering the van

- Don't forget to turn the fridge back to 240 volts or gas

Mirrors & Zones of Vision

When towing, even with the best towing mirrors available your zone of vision will be seriously reduced compared to solo driving.

The first diagram below shows the zone of vision and blind areas whilst travelling straight. There's more than enough room for a large vehicle to be hidden directly behind you as well as in the blind areas to the side.

Zones of Vision When Straight

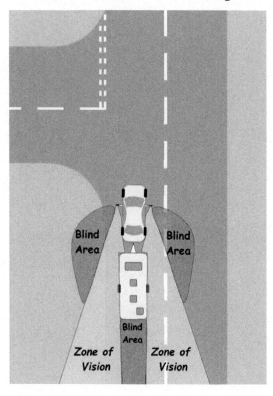

Take advantage of particularly checking the mirrors when you are going around bends where you will have a greater zone of vision on one side. Also look for shadows in your mirrors and check reflections in shop windows, both can be very useful.

The next diagram shows your zones of vision and blind areas when negotiating a left-hand corner.

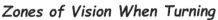

Zones of Vision When Turning

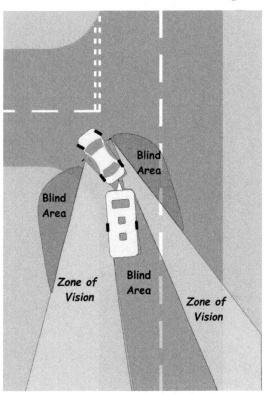

Notice that when turning left you will have no vision to the offside rear of the van at all. So, you must check this area carefully before beginning to turn - watching particularly for cyclists or overtaking vehicles. But you will have an *increased* zone of vision of the nearside.

Moving Off and Accelerating

When moving off particularly uphill you will inevitably need more revs to avoid stalling. Increasing the revs too much could damage the clutch linings, so a careful balance is needed. This is one of the reasons why diesel manuals or automatics can be preferable to petrol manuals for towing. But in all cases, you must have a tow car that is *meaty* enough for the job!

Regardless of your vehicle, due to the extra weight of the caravan it will take much longer to gather speed, consequently you will need to stay in the lower gears for longer and will also need to use the gears far more when ascending / descending hills etc.

Braking

Harsh or sudden braking is certainly not a good idea with or without a caravan on the back, but the consequences could be far worse when towing, so all the more reason for looking well ahead and keeping a safe distance from the vehicle in front - particularly in wet or windy conditions.

Braking on a bend or corner could also have disastrous consequences, so look well ahead and slow down adequately *before* bends or corners.

Another factor regarding braking whilst towing is the increased possibility of *'brake fade'*. Due to the increased weight of the van, when descending long steep hills the brakes can get very hot and ultimately fail. The way to avoid this is to stay in a lower gear in such circumstances, thus using the *'engine braking'* to reduce the strain on the brakes. There are often warning signs when this is likely to occur - *don't ignore them!*

Also, if you are in the habit of *'coasting'* downhills, I certainly wouldn't recommend this with a van on the back!

Speed Limits

Make sure that you are aware of the various speed limits for towing in the countries that you intend travelling in. The maximum in the UK is 60 mph on motorways and dual carriageways and 50 mph on single carriageways unless signs show otherwise - basically 10 mph less than for cars! But regardless of the legal limit my recommendation is always drive at a speed so that you can stop safely well within the distance that you can see to be clear having regard for the road and traffic conditions - *and speed limits!*

Snaking

Snaking is probably the biggest potential danger when towing. This is a condition when the caravan begins to swing from side to side. Once this starts, if immediate corrective action is not taken, you could lose control within seconds. The best way to correct it is to ease off the accelerator as soon as the condition begins, then slow down to a more sensible speed. Also keep the steering straight - don't try to steer out of it. It's doubtful that braking will help at all unless you're also heading into a collision.

Snaking is far more difficult to correct when traveling downhill as easing off won't necessarily slow you down. In this event gearing down could be your only option. But the most sensible way to deal with snaking is to prevent it occurring in the first place by understanding and eliminating (where possible) the causes by:

- Correct loading and *'nose weight'* as mentioned already. If there's too much weight at the back or to one side the likelihood will increase

- Make sure that the tyre pressures are correct on both van and towing vehicle

- Fit an effective stabilizer. Most new vans have an Alko stabilizer as standard, but these are only going to reduce the risk - not eliminate it. And remember these things need servicing

- Fit an ATC unit. Again, this will not eliminate the risk, but it will help

- Keep to a sensible speed, especially in wet and / or windy conditions

- Be aware of the possibility of crosswinds (covered next)

- Take notice of warning signs (particularly regarding wind and adverse cambers etc.)

- Think very carefully before overtaking anything, particularly high sided vehicles at speed - *it could be the last thing you ever do!*

Crosswinds

Due to their height and comparative light weight, caravans are particularly susceptible to problems from crosswinds. These can be caused by a *'gap'* in the terrain which is normally sheltered - i.e. a brake in a line of dense trees or buildings etc., or by other high sided vehicles, for instance when overtaking a lorry, or even when being overtaken by one.

Crossing long exposed bridges in windy conditions can also be extremely hazardous for all high sided vehicles. Often some bridges are closed to lorries and caravans when conditions are dangerous - *don't ignore the signs!*

Overtaking

Whilst towing due to your speed being comparatively reduced, it's doubtful that you will need to do a great deal of overtaking, but inevitably there will be occasions when you'll need to. In the main this will be tractors, cyclists and possibly lorries particularly on motorways and dual carriageways. It's doubtful that you'll need to overtake a many cars.

Overtaking a cyclist on a single carriageway can sometimes be more difficult than overtaking a tractor as they can often be going faster and are more unpredictable as well as far more vulnerable. But whatever you are overtaking you will need good clear vision of the road ahead for a far greater distance than when travelling solo as it will inevitably take much longer to complete the manoeuvre and return to safety. Also remember that you will need to consider your additional width and length.

Overtaking lorries etc. on motorways or dual carriageways is perhaps easier in the fact that you won't have to worry about oncoming traffic, but potentially far more dangerous due to the much higher speeds, where you may also have the problem of crosswinds as just mentioned. As a rule, it's not a bad idea to only overtake at speed when on the straight, uphill or level in good conditions. Avoid overtaking downhill or approaching bends particularly in the wet as the likelihood of snaking will increase.

In most countries the speed limit for lorries is the same as caravans and no doubt the lorries will be travelling as fast as they are permitted but may reduce speed due to lack of power when ascending hills, which can often be your best *and safest* opportunity to pass them.

In all cases use your mirrors early, change down to an appropriate gear, signal your intentions in good time and always move out (and back in) gradually. Also be aware that there could be something overtaking you which may be hidden in your blind spot!

Turning Corners

On wide roads with gradual corners towing hardly proves to be a problem as the van will simply follow the course of the tow car, although even then you must always be aware of the rear end swing and keep a keen eye on the nearside (UK) caravan wheel when turning left and the offside (UK) when turning right.

On tight corners it's a different ball game and you may well have problems, and the longer and wider the van, the more problems you are likely to have.

When turning left (UK) you may need to move over to the right to a certain degree in preparation for taking a wide path partially encroaching on the wrong side of the road that you are turning into in order to prevent the van's nearside wheel from mounting the kerb. You must also be very aware that in some cases your rear end swing (which you can't see) could cause problems to oncoming traffic in the road that you are leaving. So, in all cases take it slowly and also watch out for cyclists and motorcyclists who may attempt to pass in your nearside! Basically, take the easiest most gradual route around the corner, using whatever road space is available.

Fairly Tight Left-hand Turn

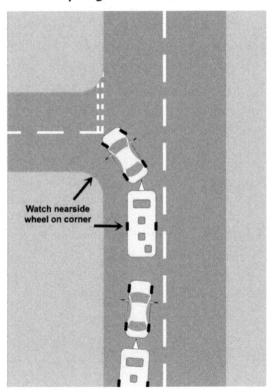

Watch nearside
wheel on corner

When turning right (UK), again you may have to take it wide, but in this case, it may involve cutting the corner and the danger of the rear end swing obliterating any cyclists attempting to pass on your nearside blind spot, so keep a keen eye out for them before they go into your blind area; and again take it slowly and steadily so that if you do hit anything, you don't hit it very hard!

Fairly Tight Right-hand Turn

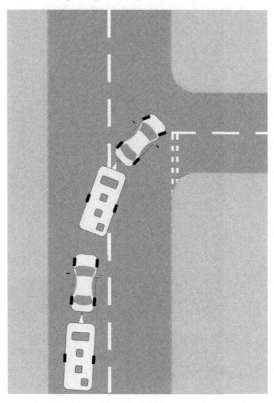

But there may be situations where you can't cut the corner, perhaps because of another vehicle waiting to emerge, or maybe a central bollard etc. In this event you will need to initially keep further to the left before turning and go further forwards than you would do normally and then turn very sharply as shown in the next diagram. But note that this will create a greater rear end swing than taking a gradual (cutting the corner) course.

Very Tight Right-hand Turn

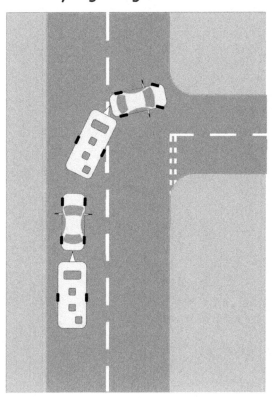

Irritatingly, the tightest corners that you are likely to encounter will be on caravan sites, particularly in the EU. You'd think that all caravan sites would be caravan friendly, but they're not! Every ACSI site that I go to, I leave a review which (among other things) always gives details of the ease of access or not as the case may be.

Motorways

If you're like most drivers, when on a motorway you will be driving at 70 mph and predominantly using the centre and offside lanes. Whilst towing it's a different *'ball game'* as your maximum speed is going to be 60 mpg (in the UK). Also remember that in the UK you are prohibited from using the third lane of a three-lane motorway whilst towing, similar to lorries.

I have to say also that it is far more difficult driving on a motorway at 60 mph than it is at 70 mph.

Why?

Because you are going to have an awful lot more traffic overtaking *you* and you will be predominantly in the first lane, occasionally using the second lane for overtaking slower lorries etc. Consequently, you will need to use your mirrors much more than when driving solo. Before changing lanes, always be aware of what may be in your blind area to the side, signal in good time and change lanes gradually. Then make sure that your caravan has cleared any vehicles in the left lane before returning.

Be particularly careful when moving into the second lane that another vehicle in the third lane is not moving into it at the same time as you - as you will both be in each other's blind spots!

If following satnav directions (particularly abroad) watch carefully for lane changes, so that they can be dealt with early. Occasionally, the satnav directions don't give enough warning in which case, stay in the lane you are in and just go the wrong way then deal with it later. I can think of one particular lane change in Lille when travelling from Belgium to France where my satnav instruction always gives insufficient time, but I'm sure there are many more. Take your time, don't do anything suddenly and keep safe!

Reversing

Ok, you've got a motor-mover, so you don't need to know how to reverse!

Wrong!

Motor-movers are brilliant and a great asset when manoeuvring your van on site or at home, but there will be times when you'll need to reverse *en-route* - hopefully not too often - but believe me it will happen. Personally, I hate these situations, but can't remember a single trip when the need has not occurred. On our last trip, one mile from our first stop-over I came to a *maximum width 6'6"* sign and had to reverse into a side road to turn around, then later I stupidly put myself in the freight lane at Euro-tunnel and had to reverse straight about 50 yards with a bunch of lorry drivers laughing at me! So, it's certainly a good idea to have some practice at reversing, preferably in an empty field or car park.

In all cases unless you have a reversing camera, you *must* have some assistance to see you back! Unfortunately, this task often becomes the wife's and it will not please her if it's humping it down with rain!

If I sound sexist here, I don't mean to be, it may well of course be the wife driving, but please forgive me as I come from an era when this was never the case and when they always used to put the dish washing facilities in the lady's toilets - *funny how times change!*

Anyway, before you start trying to reverse around corners, you will firstly need to know how to reverse straight *and keep straight.*

To begin with, try and start with the van, car and steering wheel all straight. Then begin reversing. Unless some sort of miracle occurs, it won't be long before the back end of the van begins to go off course and if left unchecked will go wildly off course. As soon as you notice this (which can be seen in the mirrors) make slight adjustment by turning the wheel slightly towards the way the van is veering, then re-adjust straight before the van starts going the other way.

Steering Adjustment when Reversing Straight

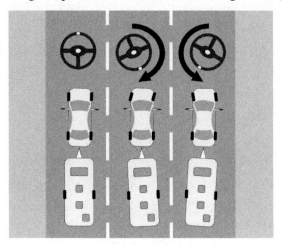

To put this another way: if the van goes to the right - *turn to the right,* if it goes to the left - *turn to the left.*

Another way of thinking this is: if you *want* the van to go to the left - *turn to the right,* if you *want* it to go to the right - *turn to the left.* Always turn the wheel the *opposite* way that you want the van to go *initially.*

Having become reasonable ok with reversing straight, you may want to have a go at reversing around a corner - with some assistance if you don't have a rear camera.

To begin with position car and van well forwards of the corner about 3' (a metre) away from the kerb. If you are too close to the kerb to begin with you will run out of space as the front of the car moves in. Then proceed as follows:

- Reverse straight until the nearside van wheel is almost at the point of turn then turn the wheel to the right - as shown in position A of the next diagram. The van will begin to go to the left - position B

- Don't keep the right lock on too long. Once the van has begun to turn, start turning the other way (to the left) - position C

- At this point the front of the car will swing well out, so be particularly careful to watch for other traffic or obstructions

- As the van reaches position D, straighten the wheel and then adjust slightly (as shown previously) to keep both van and car straight

- If it goes totally wrong at any point, you may need to pull forwards and straighten everything before re-commencing

- Most importantly - don't get flustered, if there are people waiting, let them wait and take your time

Reversing to the Left

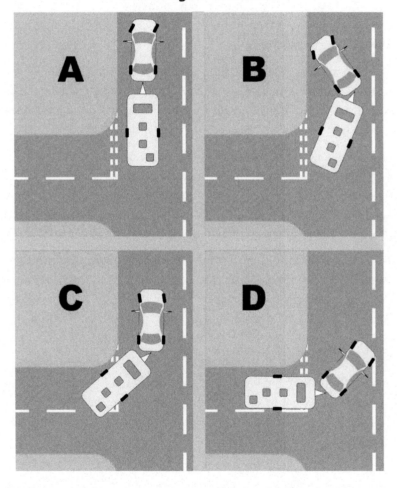

The procedure for reversing to the right (in a RHD vehicle) is of course the same, the other way around, but is possibly slightly easier as you can stick your head out of the window to see the van's wheel in relation to the kerb rather than relying on your mirror.

Incidentally reversing a short trailer is more difficult than a long one, as the short ones will *jack-knife* much sooner!

Plan Your Routes

Always plan your routes carefully according to your experience and don't over stretch yourself. Remember that when you arrive at your destination, you will need to set-up which can be a major task after a hard drive.

Also, always take adequate refreshment breaks and allow time for the unexpected. We generally aim for fours driving per day to be the maximum, although I have to say I have done a great deal more in the past. But even recently, we set out on a four-hour drive which ended up taking nine hours due to unforeseen circumstances.

It's always best to phone sites in advance to make sure that they have availability for you and also to check their opening times. Many sites in France have very long lunch breaks 12:00 - 4:00 is not unusual. It's infuriating if you've made an early start and arrive at your chosen destination to find that you have to wait two hours before you can get in!

Another thing that happens to us quite often is that our chosen destination turns out to be unsuitable and we then have to drive on much further for another. So it's always a good idea to have a *plan 'B'!*

I always keep logs of our routes across France and Spain with sites, mileages and times etc., which ae very useful to look back on when planning the next trip!

Setting Up at Your Destination

Perhaps unsurprisingly, there are a fair few things to do when arriving at your destination, some of which can be made easier with the aid of a few sensible items. In a nutshell, you will need to do the following:

- Check into the site

- Choose your pitch or drive to the one allocated for you

- Kiss the ground and give thanks that you've arrived in one piece

- If using a motor-mover, connect it at this point

- Let the cat out - *if you are blessed like us*

- Un-hitch as described previously

- Position your van with view to sunlight, shade, privacy, satellite direction and availability of electric point etc.

- Level up width-ways using a ramp if necessary

- Apply the van brakes and chock the wheels if necessary

- Level up length-ways by raising or lowering the jockey wheel

- Wind down the legs - *here the electric drill attachment will save a great deal of grief*

- Disconnect the motor-mover and isolate the switch

- Connect the 240 volts if necessary

- Fetch and connect the fresh water supply. We always carry a 10-litre bottle to avoid the initial tap hunting trip

- Connect the wastewater bottle

- Turn on the gas if necessary

- Change the fridge to 240 volts or gas

- Kettle on

Additional items such as ground sheet, awning, outside chairs etc, can be dealt with at a more leisurely pace. In our case the wind-out Fiamma blind is a Godsend as this takes literally seconds.

Hopefully you can understand the reason for not making your journey too tiring as once this lot is added to the end of it you can end up fairly knackered! And of course, if it's heaving it down with rain, you may briefly wonder why the hell you're doing any of this in the first place!

Caravan Clubs & Sites

In the UK there are two main clubs for caravans:

- the Camping and Caravanning Club
  http://www.campingandcaravanningclub.co.uk, and

- the Caravan and Motorhome Club
  https://www.caravanclub.co.uk.

Both offer a good selection of members only sites some of which are owned by the clubs, as well as low cost *'Certified Location' (CL)* sites which have limited facilities for just a few units.

Both also have local and National rallies where you can get together with other caravaners on a fairly regular basis if you are that way inclined. Personally, we don't as we mainly camp abroad. You may also find insurance and recovery cover through the clubs but do shop around elsewhere also.

We are in the Camping and Caravanning Club and the ferry discounts alone more than pays for the annual membership fees.

If you don't wish to join a club a great directory for UK campsites is: http://www.ukcampsite.co.uk/sites where you can find details of thousands of sites, also see: https://www.outandaboutlive.co.uk - click on the campsite logo.

Out of the Van Window in Brittany

Many sites allow animals and kids, but always check as some don't - more so in the UK than abroad, and also, when they state *'adults only'* be sure of the true meaning!

We once pulled into an *'adults only'* site in Spain, quite late after a hard day's drive and when enquiring if they'd got space for us, we were informed 'Yes, but we have strict rules here - you must take your clothes off!'

Now, I have absolutely no problem with people prancing about in the *nuddy* if that's what they want to do - *good luck to 'em,* although it's not normally something I'd choose to do personally. But as it was late and dark, I said to the wife, 'I'll take the dog out tonight as long as you do it in the morning!' - this was pre-cat days! Well, she wouldn't agree so we had to leave and ended up wild camping on the beach. But as we couldn't turn around, we had to drive right round the site to get out - *tits and willies everywhere!*

Ironically, the next night 300 miles away in Cadiz, a guy came up to me and said, *'I saw you last night in the naturist site!'* I didn't actually recognise him with his clothes on but thought - *'I bet I saw more of you mate!'*

ACSI

If travelling abroad or even in the UK off season, buying the ACSI books is very good sense - in fact essential - as a discount card comes with the books which gives *huge* off-season discounts at thousands of sites throughout Europe, not so many in the UK yet unfortunately, but growing. We use these on all our trips abroad and can thoroughly recommend them. See: https://www.vicarious-shop.com/ACSI-UK-CampingCard for further details.

There are also two different ACSI apps for both Android and IOS which work offline once all the sites are loaded. Although there is a small annual charge for these in addition to the books, they're both well worth having.

Both the books and the apps show details with pictures, prices and reviews of all the relevant sites along with satnav co-ordinates.

I always leave a review for all the ACSI sites that we stay at giving details of access for large units which I am always grateful to see myself.

The difference between the two apps incidentally is that the *'CC'* *(camping card)* one shows only the sites that are covered in the book which give the off-season discounts. The other one shows all the ACSI *inspected* sites, which includes the *'CC'* sites as well as many more, but for this one you have to pay for each country separately.

I always buy both apps as they're well worth the small annual fees.

Towing Tuition

Both of the caravan clubs offer towing courses for the inexperienced, which I thoroughly recommend if you've never towed before, regardless of what other driving experience you may have. A course costing a couple of hundred quid could ultimately save you a whole lot more!

Touring Abroad

We've already covered a fair few items regarding touring abroad, but here's a few more important points.

Before attempting to take a caravan abroad, make sure that you are fairly experienced at handling your unit on home turf, particularly if you have never driven abroad before.

Although all countries in mainland Europe drive on the right, it's nowhere nearly as difficult as you may imagine, particularly as most of the roads in France, Spain and Portugal are a far less crowded than the UK.

The important things to remember when driving are:

- Look *left* first at junctions or when emerging from petrol stations etc.

- Be particularly careful when leaving one-way streets, which is where you are most likely to end up on the wrong side of the road, especially when it's quiet

- Similarly, when you are on a quiet narrow road in the dark, it's all too easy to drift back to the left

- And don't forget to go around roundabouts to the right, again, you're most likely to go wrong when it's quiet

Make sure that you are aware of the driving laws in the countries that you intend travelling through - speed limits for caravans differ widely. In all cases you will need beam deflectors, but additionally you may need:

- Reflective jackets - *readily available*

- Two red triangles

- Fire extinguisher

- Two breathalysers - *in date*

- First aid kit

- Spare glasses - *if warn*

- Spare bulbs - *and the tools to fit them*

Be aware that the amount of alcohol allowed in your bloodstream is *much* lower than the UK in most EU countries. And note that you could easily be over the limit the next day after even a moderate late-night drinking session.

Petrol Stations Abroad

Generally speaking the lowest cost fuel is obtained from the supermarkets but taking a car and caravan into one of these or even many other petrol stations can be very difficult. I have never had any problems with this as I either fill up at motorway services (where there's lots of room, but you get fleeced) or ideally fill up after stopping for the night *without* the caravan attached.

In Spain incidentally, most petrol stations are very roomy and it's rarely a problem even with caravan in tow.

Specific Information for Driving in France

The French government have recently launched a new scheme for all vehicles driving in Paris and some other French cities. From 31/03/2017 your vehicle needs to display an emissions sticker showing the age and cleanliness of your vehicle.

If your vehicle does not display the sticker you could face hefty on the spot fines.

The anti-pollution sticker can be ordered on-line from the official Crit' Air website https://www.certificat-air.gouv.fr/en and will cost about £4.00. As always unscrupulous websites are selling these for overinflated prices. It's so easy that it's simply not worth not getting one.

When driving through French towns you may notice parking bays with blue lines. These are free to park in for a specific period only if you display a parking disc showing your time of arrival - similar to the UK disabled permits

The parking discs can be bought from newsagents *'maisons de presse'* or tobacconists *'tabacs'* and the price is generally under €5 euros. Failure to use the new version of the disc will result in a standard €17 parking fine - *if they can catch you!*

See: http://www.disques-de-stationnement.eu/page_2.html

Many of the EU motorways are toll roads, but as you will no doubt go through France to get to most destinations, the French ones are probably going to affect you most. We simply collect the ticket and pay at the booths with a credit / debit card which is simple as long as your card is accepted. I've had a few declined for no apparent reason, so it's a good idea to have a few different ones as we do.

You can if you wish, obtain a windscreen disc enabling you to go straight through the aisles with the 't' signs above. Then your credit card or bank will be debited automatically. I'll be honest I don't want one as I like to see what I'm paying on a moment by moment basis. See: https://www.saneftolling.co.uk for further details.

French Toll Booths

Note also that some of the pay booths have height restrictions which could affect you - very often 2m.

Switzerland & Other Tolls

If taking a vehicle into Switzerland, you will need a *'Vignette'* which costs approx. €40 per year for each vehicle (and caravan). Unfortunately, if you only want to go in for one day, you will still have to pay the yearly charge, which puts me off going there. In addition to the vignette, you will still have to pay extra for tunnels.

Similar to France, if taking a vehicle into most German towns you will need an emission sticker. These, the vignettes and toll details and tickets for many other countries are available from: https://www.tolltickets.com.

Mobile Phones

Gone are the days of public phone boxes, virtually anyway. If your vehicle breaks down or you get into bother you will need to use your mobile phone. If you haven't got the right deal it will cost you dearly, or if you use most 'pay as you go' options, you'll run out of credit before you've hardly said a word.

If you have a contract phone you may well have this sorted, but if not, you will need to think about a couple of options. Until recently (late 2019), we used 'Toggle' which was part of the 'Lyca' group which enabled very low-cost calls from abroad. But unfortunately, they closed down without warning which didn't impress me at all.

So now my advice is to buy local 'pay as you go' sim cards for the country which you're in OR use 'Skype credit' which will enable you to make low cost calls to UK landlines and mobiles from your mobile or tablet via 'Skype', but note that this does require an internet connection.

Food Abroad

At the time of writing this, most foodstuffs are more expensive throughout the EU. It's therefore sensible to take lightweight non-perishable items with you, particularly those which are either not available or grossly more expensive, - but watch the weight.

We take:

- Tea bags - *loads of them*
- Some cereals - although most are widely available
- Packets of pasta, rice, and soups
- Beans - *I need my beans!*
- Cat food - *she's a fussy cow!*
- Just a few perishables to get us going

But do always check that there are no legal restrictions regarding the import of foodstuff to the countries you wish to visit.

Without doubt at the time of writing this, Spain is far cheaper than France for groceries and eating out (and fuel). In the popular areas such as Benidorm the fierce competition keeps the prices very low.

The Lidl supermarkets are widely available throughout most EU countries and they certainly seem to be very competitive.

Language Problems

It's quite disgusting really, that I have travelled so much and can't speak more than a few words of any foreign language. But actually, a punch in the face is rarely misunderstood - *only kidding!*

The main reason that I make so little effort at languages is the fact that just about everyone else speaks English - *poor excuse I know!* But all the years that I've been travelling I've never had any great problems. I once remember trying to explain to a young waitress in Spain that I wanted *'breast'* of chicken. Well she got the idea eventually, but I seriously thought that I was going to get a punch in the face then!

Ferry Crossings

Probably the cheapest channel crossing is Dover - Calais or the Tunnel. But depending on where you live in the UK, other crossings maybe a lot more convenient. Newhaven - Dieppe with DFDS is a great crossing and they offer discounted rates for pensioners if you book directly with them and a return crossing is hardly any more than a single!

Just about all ticketing now is done with number plate recognition, so you won't need a printed ticket.

As we live in Sheffield our most convenient crossing is Hull - Zebrugge, but you have to keep an eye on the prices which vary a lot at different times and days - Saturday crossings seem to be cheapest.

When returning from Spain, although very expensive we generally use Bilbao to Portsmouth where we can get a pet cabin with the cat, but these get booked up very early. Needless to say, this can cut hundreds of miles off the total journey so part of the cost can be re-cooped by the fuel and site fees saved. Put mileage and wear and tear into the equation and it then probably actually works out cheaper.

Long Terming / Full Timing

Anyone 'long terming' or 'full timing' is most likely going to end up in Southern Spain or Portugal where the winter weather is more agreeable. There are numerous sites open all year in these areas, but many of the most convenient ones for large units get booked up very early so bear this in mind. You can usually always get on the site at Benicassim where there is a supermarket over the road and on-site entertainment all year round. There are a few sites in Benidorm which are also very convenient for winter stays - check the ACSI books to see which sites are open all year. One downside with many of the sites in convenient locations for wintering is that as space is at a premium, they tend to pack everyone in like sardines, which is why we tend to avoid them.

Note that in Portugal the *'time'* is the same as UK time, so it effectively gets dark an hour earlier than Spain which seems to bother the wife but not me - just get up an hour earlier and go to bed an hour earlier - *sorted!*

If going just for the winter or part of the winter, remember that unless you actually wait until spring to return, the roads through Central and Northern Spain can be very bad in the winter months (particularly January and February) and you may need snow chains which are obligatory on some of the Pyrenean crossings - or return via Bilbao or Santander and save yourself the grief.

Documents

When travelling abroad, be sure that your vehicle is legally insured for the countries you wish to travel to and take the documents with you including green cards if necessary.

You will also need your driving licence and vehicle registration document as well as passports for all passengers and pets.

In the event of an accident abroad you *need* a European Accident Statement form which can be downloaded from: http://cartraveldocs.com. It's not a bad idea to print out a couple of copies of these and have your details filled in just in case.

But once you have signed the form, it's binding so make sure that the other party fills in his / her part correctly before signing anything, otherwise you could inadvertently be admitting liability.

Taking Pets Abroad

Part of the great thing about camping is that you can take your pets with you - we take our cat Kizzie. But before travelling abroad your pet must be micro chipped, have the correct anti rabies injections, blood tests and pet passport. Don't leave this until the last minute as it can take months to get all this sorted out.

Our Kizzie

Additionally, dogs coming into the UK, or returning to the UK, are required to have tapeworm treatment between 1 and 5 days before entering the UK which needs to be recorded in the Pet Passport by a vet. You will therefore need to find a vet fairly near to the port you are sailing from (or the Tunnel).

When booking a ferry, you must also declare and pay for your pet. On some crossings, your pet can stay in the vehicle, on others they have to go in a cage - *like common criminals!* On the Bilbao crossings, you can get pet cabins and have them with you. Dogs have a designated exercising area, but cats need to be kept in the cabin with a litter box - we also take her scratching post, toys and reading material - *she's highly intelligent!*

Kizzie on Portsmouth - Bilbao Ferry

See: https://www.gov.uk/government/organisations/department-for-environment-food-rural-affairs (DEFRA) for the most up to date official information.

Banks

It's a good idea to let your bank and credit card companies know that you are travelling abroad and for some this is a requirement.

Also make a note of all your bank and credit card account numbers etc. (not pin numbers) and contact details, so that you can contact them in case of emergency. All the relevant details are printed on the cards, which is not much good to you if you lose them or have them stolen - so always keep them separate - *I use MS OneNote!*

Be particularly vigilant when using credit cards; do not let them out of your sight, as once the card number and the security number on the back falls into the wrong hands these can be used for internet purchases. This once happened to us, although we were in England at the time. Fortunately, the bank picked up on it pretty quick.

Another thing that happened once was that I paid a restaurant bill with a debit card, put in the pin number and was then informed that transaction had failed - as the machine curiously broke down at that moment, so I also paid in cash. After checking my bank, it showed that the transaction *had* gone through, but fortunately I managed to get it cancelled.

Newspapers Abroad

The cost of buying English newspapers abroad (when available) is totally crazy. But the wife likes her Daily Mail - *newspaper that is*. Our solution is to get the digital version for £11 month - you also get a month's free trial. To get this you will of course need an internet connection. We've also tried the Daily Express, which is a little cheaper, but the crosswords didn't work - maybe they do now! No doubt there are others.

Winterising Your Unit

Whether you have a caravan, folding camper, static or motorhome, they all need winterising when not in use in potential freezing temperatures.

You should of course always follow the manufacturer's advice on this, but it basically entails:

- First and foremost, in all cases the boiler needs to be drained which is normally done by opening a small drain tap (most seem to be yellow)

- Open all taps to drain and leave mixer taps open between hot and cold - don't forget the shower even if you don't use it!

- Drain cold water storage tanks

- Additionally, you could air blow all water pipes to get rid of every drop of water, but to be honest I've never done this

- Drain wastewater tanks

- Drain the toilet flush

- Empty and clean the toilet

- Cover the boiler and fridge vents

- Clean the fridge and leave the door OPEN

- Clean the inside of the van thoroughly including and especially inside all lockers to remove *all* traces of food

- Set mouse traps with chocolate as bait - if you do have any trouble with mice, they can cause havoc, so make regular checks

- Turn the 12v supply off. Ideally occasionally connect the 240v lead if possible, to keep the leisure battery topped up. *A solar panel does a good job here*

- If possible, use a dehumidifier inside during the cold periods. If an electric one is impossible use the crystal type and renew them as required

- A breathable external cover could be also a good idea if you need to store your van under a tree that drops sap etc., but this will disable the solar panel. We had one once and to be honest, *I'd rather polish the roof than go through the hassle!*

Clearly the bigger and more complicated the unit the more things there are to do and to forget, so a printed check list can be very useful.

I once forgot to open a tap in the Hymer, which basically cost me a tap! We've also had trouble with a mouse, but one that the cat brought in and dropped while we were using it. I tried to catch it alive, but sadly had to kill it in the end - *after three months of trying!*

Selling Your Van

Whatever van you end up buying, it's inevitable that at some point you will eventually sell it. If you always have this in mind when buying, your losses can be minimised.

Needless to say, how well you look after your van and how well you present it for sale will be major factors in the selling price that you finally achieve. But unless you initially buy pre-owned very astutely, you've got to accept the fact that it will depreciate!

As previously mentioned, we keep the original carpets and cushions in the house unused and keep the seats covered when in use so that the interior is as pristine as can be when it comes to selling. I regularly wash and polish the exterior and have the van serviced in accordance with the manufacturer's stipulations, which ensures that any existing warranties can be transferred to the new owners. It's not always necessary to go back to the selling agent for servicing, but in most cases, you will need to use an NCC approved workshop - we use a mobile guy, who is good, economical and comes to us!

Prepare Your Van for Selling

I know this may seem like I'm *'stating the bleeding obvious'* but prepare your van by thoroughly cleaning it inside and out, including all lockers and toilet etc. Carry out any remedial work that's necessary. This done take photos inside and out to the best of your ability showing any flaws if applicable - there's no point in trying to hide anything!

Make a list of all the good points, specifications and extras (motor-mover, awning etc.) to assist in writing your advert. Look at similar vans for sale to help gauge your starting price which should allow a little *'wiggle room'*. Also check out the dealers to see what they are selling similar for. Setting a fair price will ensure a sale but remember condition matters!

When you are fully prepared, you will need to place adverts in suitable media such as:

- eBay *classified* adverts
- Gumtree *(free)*
- Preloved *(free)*
- Facebook - *Marketplace (free)*
- Caravan magazines

We've always had success with one of the top three. The downside with caravan magazines is that you have to wait several weeks for the publication and they also tend to be very expensive. Note that eBay classified is not the same as the auction, which you could of course use if you so wish. The classified adverts enable you to sell at a fixed price and pay eBay a fixed fee for a set period. This way you will have huge exposure for a very reasonable price and there will be no further fees to pay when you find a buyer (unlike the auction fees).

Use common sense when receiving payment. I only accept either cash or bank transfers which must be in my bank before the van leaves me. Avoid cheques or bank drafts (many are forged). Bank transfers are the only really safe way as even cash can be forged!

Stress that the buyer must collect and arrange insurance and suitable tow car, mirrors and number plate.

Provide the buyer with the VIN No. before completing so that he / she can arrange insurance cover.

When the sale is complete (not before), sign the CRIS document and pass this to the new owner for him to register.

I always give the new owner a computer written receipt stating that the van is sold as seen and inspected with no known faults, but without warranty (unless one is still valid) and that there is no outstanding finance owed on the van. I also give the new owner all the relevant service history and receipts for extras etc.

But most importantly, consider any problems you may have selling your caravan *on the day you buy it!* You never own anything permanently (apart from maybe your toothbrush) - you are just a temporary keeper! So, buy carefully, look after your investment and sell wisely, thus minimising your losses.

Insurance

Back in the 60's / 70's when I was a touring musician, I used to travel the length and breadth of Europe with nothing more than the legal insurance requirements - no breakdown cover - no medical insurance, well before we joined the EU, and I never even considered the possible consequences. Such is youth.

These days I'm more cautious and want to cover every eventuality - but it's not easy. There are so many different policies with so many *ifs, ands and buts* in the small print.

Ok, so let's look at what you need and probably want if you are sensible:

- Vehicle insurance
- Caravan insurance
- Breakdown and recovery for all vehicles
- Sickness Insurance
- Pet insurance - *if necessary*
- Home Insurance cover while you are absent

Car Insurance

No doubt you have your car covered for the UK but check that you are you are comprehensively insured for the countries that you intend travelling to. This may well all be covered within your existing policy, but usually only for a certain number of consecutive days - so check! If you are going to Andorra or Monaco, double check as they are often excluded.

If towing a caravan or trailer, this should be covered for third part liability on your car insurance, *as long as you declared the tow bar as a modification!* If you want comprehensive cover for the caravan, this must be taken out separately. You may need a green card for both car *and* caravan if travelling abroad - check with your insurance company.

Caravan Insurance

The price of caravan insurance can vary widely (like car insurance) as it's generally based on your post code, previous claims, experience, unit value and place of storage etc. Check also the number of consecutive days that you can use it abroad if this is your intention.

I wouldn't normally recommend any insurance company as we've had so many not so good ones, but for our latest van we are using https://www.caravanguard.co.uk who I have to say are excellent. They are clearly a specialist company who really seem to care about their customers and give a great deal of ongoing advice, information and newsletters. Before signing up with them I checked many other companies for prices etc. and can confirm that they are very competitive, in fact probably the best value when considering *'like for like'* cover. They also give genuine discounts for any security and safety items as well as no claims discounts.

Make a note of the van's VIN number, shipping length (the total length including the A-frame), height and width as you will need this information for insurance, recovery insurance as well as ferry crossings etc.

Breakdown Recovery Insurance

Although not compulsory, you would be somewhat irresponsible to travel without vehicle breakdown / recovery / repatriation cover for your car and caravan. The caravan may be covered on your car EU recovery, but only if it is attached to the car at the time of breakdown and only as long as it falls within the length, width and height stipulations. 7m is usually the longest for standard cover which is available through *'Green Flag'*. If your van is longer you will need to look further. The caravan clubs are a good starting point. But some banks also offer good EU recovery deals to include your caravan but be sure to read the small print.

Travel Insurance

There are many companies offering travel insurance, either just for a fixed trip, or on an annual basis, but in all cases read the small print carefully as some are vastly superior to others.

In this case some banks offer reasonable deals. We're with the Nationwide and get free cover for a certain period and only pay a small additional payment for extended trips despite the wife's blood pressure and *compulsive cleaning disorder.*

Finally, what if the only driver gets taken ill and can't drive the car / caravan back to the UK? Your vehicle recovery / repatriation will not cover you unless the cause is a breakdown. Your vehicle comprehensive insurance policy won't cover you unless the driver became ill as a result of an accident in the vehicle. Your health insurance may well repatriate the driver and maybe even the spouse - but who brings the car and caravan back?

With this in mind I did find a quite expensive travel insurance that covered this eventuality and we used them for a few years. Then one day in a fit of boredom I read the small print and discovered to my horror that they would only pay a maximum of £1,000 *towards* recovery in this event.

I investigated further to find out exactly how much it could cost to have a car and caravan repatriated from say Barcelona to Sheffield. At the time which was a few years ago this was about £4,000 from http://normanmarshall.co.uk who seem to be the only people who do it. So actually, this very expensive policy hardly covered us at all - so I cancelled it and remain un-insured for this hopefully unlikely eventuality. But I shall continue to look for this cover as I believe it to be important, especially for us *wrinklies!*

Home Insurance

No doubt you have your home insured for buildings and contents cover, although there are no laws or rules insisting that you have to unless your property is mortgaged. But in every case, there will be a clause in the policy stating that you must not leave the property uninhabited for longer than a certain period - ours is 60 consecutive days. We get around this with the help of a relative who inhabits it for us for one day and then the 60 days start again, but there are usually stipulations whereby they must actually eat and sleep there!

We also have video cameras in some of our rooms that automatically record any activity, and then alerts us so that we can see this online. This gives us peace of mind knowing that all is well at home. See: https://home.nest.com.

Another point to remember is that if you keep your caravan at home as we do, it's blatantly obvious that you are away when the unit is missing. So far, where we live now this hasn't been a problem, but at a previous house, the place was broken into repeatedly when we were away, despite gate locks, alarms, security lighting and the best locks available, they just smashed the glass and walked in! The police told us that there was absolutely nothing else that we could do about it.

Pet Insurance

If you are taking a pet with you as we do, beyond all the injections, blood tests etc. that will be necessary you would be wise to have pet medical insurance. Your existing pet insurance may well cover you, but possibly only for a certain amount of days as ours does. In our case this is not extendable, so we take out separate short-term cover with E&L which is quite useful to know. See: https://www.eandl.co.uk for further information.

Kizzie - In Attack Mode

Thank You

Well, that's it folks! But last but not least I'd like to thank you kindly for buying this book. It's been my sincere wish to provide more value in real terms than the cost of this book. I hope that you think that I've succeeded, if so, I would be very grateful if you'd consider leaving me a review with a few kind words on Amazon, Lulu etc., or from wherever you made your purchase.

I can be contacted at the contact pages of any of my websites listed on the next page.

Kind Regards and thanks again,

Martin

Download Link

If you have the paperback version, you can freely download the digital PDF version at:

http://deep-relaxation.co.uk/caravanning_dl.html.

But please honour my copyright by using this for your own use only - thank you!

Final Word

Don't forget to keep your mouth shut when you empty your chemical toilet!

Disclaimer

Although the author and publisher have made every effort to ensure that the information in this book was correct at the time of press, the author and publisher do not assume and hereby disclaim any liability to any party for any loss, damage, or disruption caused by errors or omissions, whether such errors or omissions result from negligence, accident, or any other cause.

And the suggestion that you should kill the tradesman who fits your safe is a joke and not to be taken literally!

Other Books by Martin Woodward

- Use Your Mind to Learn How to Drive

- Clutch Control & Gears Explained

- The Golden Sphere - An Introduction to Rebirthing and A Course in Miracles

- Brainwave Entrainment Plus ♫

- Relaxation CD's & mp3 Recordings ♫

See: http://deep-relaxation.co.uk for details of the above

- Learn How to Play Electronic Keyboard / Piano in a Week! ♫

- Keyboard Improvisation One Note at a Time ♫

- Learn How to Play Piano / Keyboard for Absolute Beginners ♫

- Learn How to Play Piano / Keyboard By Ear! ♫

- Learn How to Play Piano / Keyboard With Filo & Pastry ♫

- New Easy Original Piano / Keyboard Music ♫

- Plus several others

See: http://learn-keyboard.co.uk for details of the above

Printed in Great Britain
by Amazon

77188073R00078